A special gift from
Mazda Motor of America, Inc.

mazda
IT JUST FEELS RIGHT.

The Meaning of Life

Reflections in Words and Pictures on Why We Are Here

David Friend
and the Editors of

LITTLE, BROWN AND COMPANY
BOSTON TORONTO LONDON

Library of Congress Cataloging-in-Publication Data

The Meaning of life: reflections in words and pictures on why we are
    here/David Friend and the Editors of *Life*.
            p.   cm.
    ISBN 0-316-29402-0
    1. *Life*. 2. Celebrities—Interviews.   I. Friend, David. 1955–
II. *Life* (Chicago, Ill.: 1978)
BD431.M46885   1991
128—dc20   89-27269
                                             CIP

10 9 8 7 6 5 4 3 2

*We are grateful to Basic Books, Inc., for permission
to quote from* Alvarez: Adventures of a Physicist
*by Luis W. Alvarez (New York: Basic Books, 1987).
Carl Sagan contribution © Carl Sagan*

BP

Published simultaneously in Canada
by Little, Brown & Company (Canada) Limited
PRINTED IN THE UNITED STATES OF AMERICA

Acknowledgments

This book could never have been produced without the intuition and persistence of former LIFE Managing Editor Pat Ryan and the courageous good will of Little, Brown's Publisher Roger Donald and Editor-in-Chief William Phillips. LIFE Managing Editor Jim Gaines also provided generous support.

The Meaning of Life was designed with the conviction and, I would even say, enlightenment of Tom Bentkowski, LIFE's Director of Design. Linda Ferrer served as Picture Editor, helping me choose the photographers and images that eventually made it into the book. The chief workhorses responsible for contacting and, at times, interviewing respondents for their contributions were reporters Karen Emmons, Jennifer Gilliland, Linda Gomez and Peter Meyer. Reporting assistance was augmented by LIFE bureau staffs and stringers and by Time-Life News Service personnel in eight countries. Copy editing was a labor of love, patience and vision, courtesy of Paula Glatzer, LIFE's Copy Chief.

For his encouragement, tutelage and advice, I have to thank one of the world's greatest photographers and friends, Harry Benson. Along with Harry, photographers John Loengard and Bob Adelman, and LIFE Picture Editor Bobbi Baker Burrows, withstood many hours of badgering and provided important insights that shaped the book. Armour Craig and John Frook helped in ways they'll never know.

Invaluable advice was also provided by Editorial Director of Time Inc. Magazines Richard Stolley, LIFE Assistant Managing Editors Jay Lovinger and Mary Steinbauer, LIFE Director of Photography Peter Howe, Cornell Capa and Willis Hartshorn of the International Center of Photography, Ron Benenati, formerly of New York Open Center, and James Parks Morton, dean of the Cathedral of St. John the Divine in Manhattan.

Others who helped make this book possible were: Joe Aprea, Frank Ashley, Eric Berk, Pam Bernstein, Joshua Bilmes, Katherine Bonniwell, Toni Burbank, David Carey, Clayton Carlson, Susan Caughman, Howard Chapnick (Black Star), Peter Christopoulous, Debra Cohen, Karen Dane, Robert Dannin (Magnum Photos), Lisa Distelheim, Mary Doherty, Christina Eckerson, Laury Frieber, Jane Furth, Elizabeth Gallin, June Goldberg, Marti Golon, Megan Gray, Bob Gurbani, Lynn Hale, Susan Hayes, Brendan Keenan, Hans Kohl, Carol LaRusso, Nan Leonard, Kevin Lewis, Barbara Maddux, Elaine Markson, Marlene McCampbell, Marilyn McGuire (New Age Publishing and Retailing Alliance), Wib Middleton, Roger Neal, Larry Nesbitt, Irene Neves, Frank Perich, Françoise Piffard, Robert Pledge (Contact Press Images), Ronald Precht, Carmine Romanelli, Joshua Simon, Bonnie J. Smith, Jeffrey Smith, Hal Stall, Anna Stewart, John Taylor, Cornelis Verwaal, Gretchen Wessels and Beth Benzine Zarcone.

Finally, inspiration was supplied in various forms by my ever understanding wife, Nancy Paulsen, and the following: the Adasheks, Sue Allison, Jane Amsterdam, Jeffrey Atkin, Jonathan Bender, Janet and Steve Berman, Pete Bonventre, Todd Brewster, John Bryson, David Burton, Bob Ciano, Jeffrey Claman, George Howe Colt, Tod Cooper, Brad Darrach, Anne de Flumeri, Gedeon de Margitay, Sheila Dekel, Andrew Eichner, Anne Fadiman, Leonard Fein, Ellen and Martin Friend, Richard and Sadie Friend, Donald Garber, Murray Goldwaser, Rita Healy, Dan Higgins, Tom Higgins, Jeffrey Hogan, Jim Kamin, David Kirsh, Mark Kotfila, Marc Kravitz, Brian Lanker, Jon Larsen, Betsy Lembeck, James Mendelsohn, Michael Mendelsohn, David Moore, Ann Morrell, Bill Moyers, Amy and Bert Nalle, Barry O'Connell, Dan Okrent, Brad and Cathy Paulsen, Joe and Ann Paulsen, Steve Petranek, Joe Poindexter, Steve Robinson, Joann and Michael Rooney, Roy Rowan, Peggy Samuels, Marie Schumann, Lester Schwalb, Harriet Seitler, Henry Shaw, the Silvermans, Al and Kay Simons, Riley Steiner, Carrie Tuhy, Eleanor Van Bellingham, Chris Whipple, Elie Wiesel, Bruce Wolf, Maharishi Mahesh Yogi. And Sam and Molly.

—D. F.

EDITOR David Friend

DIRECTOR OF DESIGN Tom Bentkowski

PICTURE EDITOR Linda Ferrer

REPORTERS Karen Emmons
Jennifer Gilliland
Linda Gomez
Peter Meyer

COPY CHIEF Paula Glatzer

CORRESPONDENTS (London)
Nicholas Lequesne,
Liz Nickson,
Gail Ridgwell
(Paris)
Tala Skari, Hélène Veret
(Rome)
Mimi Murphy
(Moscow)
Kanta Stanchina
(Tokyo)
S. Chang
(Bonn)
Dorothea Ramroth
(Quito)
Maria Helena Jervis
(Chicago)
Jack Hayes, Donald Liebenson
(Los Angeles)
James Grant, Jennifer Ash
(Miami)
Valerie Gladstone
(St. Louis)
Staci Kramer

RESEARCH Jacqueline Coleman

PICTURE REPORTERS Tina Clark
Steve Freeman
Kathi Kosiancic
Dolores Metzner

COPY DEPARTMENT Ricki Tarlow
Jean Taylor

DESIGN ASSISTANT Mimi Park

Alfred Eisenstaedt
CURIOSITY

Introduction

Yogis ponder the question on lofty cliffs. Theologians and clergymen study it and rephrase it and return to it again and again. Comedians have a field day with it.

What is the meaning of life?

In 1988 the editors of LIFE magazine decided to be characteristically shameless. We attempted to tackle the question head-on and asked some fifty wise men and women from all walks of life—from the Dalai Lama to civil rights pioneer Rosa Parks—to offer short responses to the admittedly audacious query. We then asked photographers to submit pictures that, to them, captured a bit of the essence of existence in a single photographic frame. The resulting article, an award-winning collection of essays and photos, received such a positive reaction from our readers and colleagues that we have now expanded it into this volume.

The Meaning of Life is the product of 300 thoughtful people. First, it is a compendium of observations from 173 poets and scientists, artists and statesmen, philosophers and everyday sages on the street. The responses, all written specifically at LIFE magazine's request, are succinct. Most run no longer than 250 words. And though the contributors hail from more than 25 countries, they are people whose work or outlook, as a rule, appeals to LIFE's audience: Most have a decidedly American sensibility or maintain some connection with American popular culture.

The words are complemented by pictures from 127 of the world's top photographers. A good many have appeared in the pages of LIFE. Of the remainder, most were submitted by the photographers, though many were selected from portfolios after photographers deferred to us with something along these lines: "The meaning of life? C'mon. *You* pick a picture!" Finally, a handful of photos are here simply because we couldn't resist them. We stumbled across them or had enjoyed them for years or found them particularly refreshing and inspirational in the context of this book—and felt we couldn't produce *The Meaning of Life* without them. Uplifting and unsettling by turns, the images, when taken together, stand as a testament to the belief that the medium of photography is unmatched in its ability to convey the most profound and powerful messages of our time.

Like all wild ideas, *The Meaning of Life* has had its share of naysayers. In 1985 I was covering news stories for LIFE, soon to become the news editor of the monthly magazine. But from time to time my attention would stray to less pressing subjects. And during one editorial meeting I found myself contemplating LIFE's red-and-white logo, wondering: What better cover line than "The Meaning of Life"? Why not try to canvass some of the world's less ignorant men and women to come up with a few answers?

My notion was drowned out with loud if good-natured laughter. Yet I pursued the idea for the next three years at a succession of story conferences, suggesting it meekly, sometimes pretending I was only joking. Finally, in the fall of 1988, Pat Ryan, then LIFE's Managing Editor—smitten with the spirit of the upcoming holiday season—decided to give it a try for a December cover.

After the piece was published, many observed: "Isn't it odd that no one has done this before?" In fact, many have. As I discovered while editing this book, philosopher Will Durant produced *On the Meaning of Life* in 1932, publishing quips from two dozen of his contemporaries (from mathematician-philosopher Bertrand Russell to life-term convict 79206 at Sing-Sing prison). More recently, there have been anthologies like Jon Winokur's *Zen to Go* and, as luck would have it, *The Meaning of Life*, a slim treasury of famous authors' musings (actually hand-written inscriptions) collected over 35 years by philosopher and autograph hound Hugh S. Moorhead.

Nonetheless, I proceeded with this book, convinced that many would-be sages would find virtue in attempting to answer this weighty question, no matter how hackneyed or cockeyed it all sounded when first explained over the telephone. Not so. Initially, turndowns came at a breakneck pace. Nobel Prize-winning economist Milton Friedman declined graciously, explaining, "I never comment on anything I don't know about." So, too, I. M. Pei, whose assistant apologized that the architect couldn't cooperate since he was "booked up for the next two years." Sociologist Daniel Bell offered one of the best rebuffs: "The idea of such a symposium is cockamamy. Two kinds of people will read it. One group is wide-eyed and amazed and they are fools. The other group will read it and say to themselves, *These* guys are fools.' " In all, some 650 people were approached by LIFE staffers in order to come up with the contributions that appear here.

Responses varied enormously. Avant-garde composer John Cage sent a four-word telegram. The Dalai Lama, the exiled Tibetan Buddhist leader, submitted four typewritten pages. (When another contributor, counterculture guru Ram Dass, heard that I had taken on the unenviable task of condensing the Dalai Lama's response to 250 words, he blanched: "Tough job, editing God.")

Performers wrote songs. Poets wrote prose. Contributors fidgeted by candlelight, by word processor, by secretary. Though some agreed to lengthy telephone interviews (that were then edited down and read back to them and reworked once more), most sent along written responses. And many mornings I would find my in-box brimming with postcards and blurry photocopies. One afternoon, four days after I had requested disciples of Hindu mystic J. P. Vaswani to track him down, Vaswani's entry (written on a mountain peak in India) arrived in my Manhattan office—by fax.

Certain participants went to great lengths to be included in the book. Several chose to respond the same week that a close relative had passed away. Michael Harrington, the esteemed Socialist thinker and author, composed his piece at his doctor's, between treatments for the cancer that subsequently claimed his life. Photographer Robert Mapplethorpe's haunting submission arrived from his studio the day before his death. Jazzman Dexter Gordon, photographer Ethan Hoffman and rabbi Wolfe Kelman also passed on after offering their contributions. And Nobel physicist Luis Alvarez died only a week after agreeing to submit a response. Peter Trower, a close friend of Alvarez's, sent along this note: "Tomorrow I scatter his ashes beyond the Golden Gate Bridge. . . . What I offer is the best I can do from the man who witnessed the first two atomic bomb drops." He enclosed this excerpt from the book *Alvarez: Adventures of a Physicist:*

> [A]ny Supreme Being must have been a great mathematician. The universe operates with precision according to mathematical laws of enormous complexity. I'm unable to identify its creator with the Jesus to whom my maternal grandparents, missionaries in China, devoted their lives. . . . To me the idea of a Supreme Being is attractive, but I'm sure that such a Being isn't the one described in any holy book.

His words and his death serve as humbling reminders of the brief span during which we can ponder this eternal question.

—David Friend

Ken Heyman
NEWARK, NEW JERSEY

(Overleaf)
Alfred Eisenstaedt
PUPPET SHOW, "THE DRAGON IS SLAIN"

The Old Testament Book of Micah answers the question of why we are here with another question: "What doth the Lord require of thee but to do justly, and to love mercy, and to walk humbly with thy God?"

We are here to witness the creation and to abet it. We are here to notice each thing so each thing gets noticed. Together we notice not only each mountain shadow and each stone on the beach but, especially, we notice the beautiful faces and complex natures of each other. We are here to bring to consciousness the beauty and power that are around us and to praise the people who are here with us. We witness our generation and our times. We watch the weather. Otherwise, creation would be playing to an empty house.

According to the second law of thermodynamics, things fall apart. Structures disintegrate. Buckminster Fuller hinted at a reason we are here: By creating things, by thinking up new combinations, we counteract this flow of entropy. We make new structures, new wholenesses, so the universe comes out even. A shepherd on a hilltop who looks at a mess of stars and thinks, "There's a hunter, a plow, a fish," is making mental connections that have as much real force in the universe as the very fires in those stars themselves.

Annie Dillard,
Pulitzer Prize-winning essayist, poet and teacher, is the author of *Pilgrim at Tinker Creek*.

Nubar Alexanian
LANDSCAPE, CHINCEROS, PERU

Challenger 6, 41 G
Space Shuttle Crew/NASA
CUMULONIMBUS CLOUDS OVER
CENTRAL NIGERIA

The evolution of the world is a great manifestation of God. As scientists understand more and more about the interdependence not only of living things but of rocks, rivers—the *whole* of the universe—I am left in awe that I, too, am a part of this tremendous miracle. Not only am I a part of this pulsating network, but I am an indispensable part. It is not only theology that teaches me this, but it is the truth that environmentalists shout from the rooftops. Every living creature is an essential part of the whole.

All creatures have special attributes. Our particular attribute is the ability to reason. With reason we are enabled to react independently from our environment. What are we supposed to do?

Our surroundings are awesome. We see about us majestic mountains, the perfection of a tiny mouse, a newborn baby, a flower, the colors of a seashell. Each creature is most fully that which it is created to be, an almost incredible reflection of the infinite, the invisible, the indefinable. All women and men participate in that reflected glory.

We believe that we are in fact the image of our Creator. Our response must be to live up to that amazing potential—to give God glory by reflecting His beauty and His love. That is why we are here and that is the purpose of our lives. In that response we enter most fully into relationships with God, our fellow men and women, and we are in harmony with all creation.

Desmond Tutu,

South African civil rights leader and Nobel Peace Prize winner, is the Anglican Archbishop of Capetown.

A man is mortal while mankind is not. I trust that believers and nonbelievers alike recognize this. Like a human embryo that evolves through all stages of evolution, the human spirit repeats the cosmic history of mankind in its microcosmic development, thus binding the past and the future. This deep bind, this intertwining of cosmic and microcosmic development within each human being, shapes the meaning of life and its values. In fact, life's meaning and life's values are more precious than life itself.

Mankind's technological evolution, primarily the development of nuclear weapons, has now deprived mankind of immortality. As the cancer cells of nuclear arms have already yielded powerful metastases in certain countries and across national boundaries, our generation faces perhaps its greatest task: eliminating those seeds of destruction and restoring mankind to immortality. The experience gained through that joint mission will help us to realize life's meaning and the ways of handling other threats to life on this planet, brought forth through the aggregated activities of man.

Yevgeni Velikov,

physicist and key adviser on arms control and science issues to Soviet leader Mikhail Gorbachev, is the vice president of the Soviet Academy of Sciences and chairman of the International Foundation for the Survival and Development of Humanity.

We human beings are only one small part of creation. Sometimes we act as if we were the whole rather than merely a part of creation. There are other worlds besides the human world. The plant world and the animal world are equally important parts of this creation.

The meaning of life is to live in balance and harmony with every other living thing in creation. We must all strive to understand the interconnectedness of all living things and accept our individual role in the protection and support of other life forms on earth. We must also understand our own insignificance in the totality of things.

Wilma Mankiller,

chief of the Cherokee Nation, is the first woman to lead a large Native American tribe.

As we travel in space we can see more clearly that we enjoy a unique experience as living creatures. We are part of the cavalcade of life on this special planet; we can rejoice in the gift of life. Whether this gift originated with an "unmoved first mover" is a metaphysical riddle. But we need not search too far to find godlike powers in the universe today. We as a species are exerting them now in a display unprecedented since creation began.

Homo sapiens has appropriated two thirds of the land of the planet, destroying the habitat for millions of other species and extinguishing them. As this millennium ends, the technology of industrialism has damaged the ozone shield for all life and has triggered an epochal change in global climate. We are not immortal, but our acts are.

Our species is acting like gods using primal powers to reorder the universe, but who would claim that we have the wisdom, let alone the right, to do so? We are doing this for our uses alone. The rights and needs of our co-venturers on this planet are not even acknowledged.

The question is not why we exist but whether we deserve to exist as supposedly rational beings if we act like conquerors rather than caring beings willing to share the planet with all those who are less powerful, and to act with restraint in respecting the needs of others and all life to come. As a species, we are on trial to see whether rationality was an advance or a tragic mistake.

Michael McCloskey,

environmentalist and attorney, is chairman of the Sierra Club.

Lennart Nilsson
EIGHTEEN-WEEK-OLD HUMAN-TO-BE

Robert Mapplethorpe
LISA LYON WITH CAPE AND CRYSTAL BALL

I do not think that one can talk about life without talking about death. I believe in life after death. Without such a belief I would find life in this world very difficult and meaningless. I worry at times that my belief in the afterlife might be a cop-out. Such a belief can never become the excuse for not being involved in the struggle for understanding our present existence, for not trying to achieve some fulfillment, for not working for a more just, free and participative society throughout our globe. Life in this world is a very important reality, but it is not the ultimate reality.

In this world love of God, love of neighbor and love of self go together. In practice we are all aware of the dangers of an excessive love of self. There is also truth in the paradox that only in giving do we receive. But I believe there is a proper love of self that is compatible with love of God and love of neighbor, near and far. True growth in this world always calls for a dying to my own sinfulness, individualism and selfishness so that I might come closer to my true self in relationship to all others and to God.

Thus, in the end, life and death are not diametrically opposed. Life involves a dying and dying is a way to life.

Charles Curran,

Catholic theologian, has been censured by the Vatican for his views on various issues of sexual ethics.

Almost every day of my life I see people in the process of going from the diagnosis of a dread disease to a terminal stage in that disease. Having encountered so many people facing the end of life, having witnessed them and their loved ones as they've asked, in an urgent and profound way, "What has *my* life meant?" I feel I have some partial answer to the reason we all exist. I am led to believe that if there is a real purpose for any of us, it is to somehow enhance each other's humanity— to love, to touch others' lives, to put others in touch with basic human emotions, to know that you have made even one life breathe easier because you have lived. By and large, the meaning of a person's life gets distilled to: How well have I loved? A person can then find hope in believing: Somebody loved me and I loved him or her and those memories that my loved one carries forward will shimmer on inside my children and grandchildren and beyond. When I talk to elderly people who are dying, if they have any regrets, they don't worry about their lack of material gain or about having had too little success in life. They worry about the kind of things they didn't do and should have done with the people that they loved.

I remember an unmarried teacher who was dying. She realized her life had been rich because, as she told me, "I know I've touched other people's lives and their lives are better for having known me." And there was a merchant seaman dying of gastric cancer that had been diagnosed at a late stage. He regretted that he had never married. But as we talked, he revealed that he had had many friends. He had traveled a lot. In sorting through the riffraff, he was able to find meaning in his life by virtue of the fact that he felt he had instilled a sense of passion for the experience of life within the souls of the people that he had known.

People sometimes ask me how I get through it all. I cry a lot. I love the people, I grieve their loss and I go on to the next one.

Leah de Roulet,

social worker, counsels terminal cancer patients and their families.

My wife died of bone cancer sixteen years ago. In her dying hours she went over the plans for my professional, domestic and marital future. She reviewed the best ways our three teenage sons could cope with losing her. She arranged how her father should be told of her death. We talked over the three serious quarrels we'd had in twenty years of married life. She wanted no unfinished business.

Having taken care of everyone else as best she could, she felt entitled to the ultimate act of personal choice: She took an overdose and died in my arms. The manner of her dying showed me that the meaning of life is consideration for others at all times, through human love and comradeship. Until then I had not understood the practical implications of caring.

Derek Humphry,

British right-to-die activist, is executive director of the Hemlock Society.

Grey Villet
FAITH

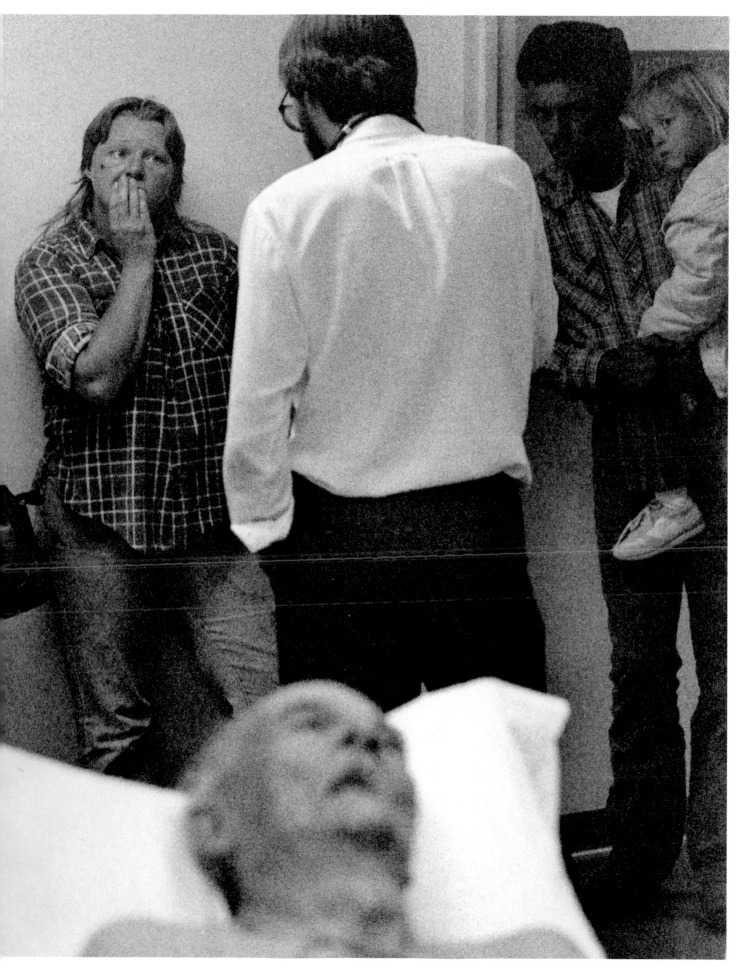

The meaning of life is listening to Pavarotti, feeling the sun on your face, drinking a bottle of wine, and then another. The meaning of life is having a safe and healthy society, a happy family life, good health, a loving wife, work that you like, smelling the smell of a new car and the ocean air, being able to hit a bull's-eye, coming home with the fish and not another fish story.

Carmine Pucci
is a butcher.

Vsevolod Tarasevich
THE GOLDEN KISS, SIBERIA

Since age two I've been waltzing up and down with the question of life's meaning. And I am obliged to report that the answer changes from week to week. When I know the answer, I know it absolutely; as soon as I know that I know it, I know that I know nothing. About seventy percent of the time my conclusion is that there is a grand design. I believe that the force that created life is betting that human beings will do something quite wonderful—like live up to their potential. I am influenced largely by Blaise Pascal and his wager. Pascal advises us to bet on the toss of a coin that God *is*. If we win, we win eternity. If we lose, we lose nothing.

I'm looking out a large window now and I see about forty dogwood and maple and oak and locust trees and the light is on some of the leaves and it's so beautiful. Sometimes I'm overcome with gratitude at such sights and feel that each of us has a responsibility for being alive: one responsibility to creation, of which we are a part, another to the creator—a debt we repay by trying to extend our areas of comprehension.

Maya Angelou,
writer and actress, is the author of
I Know Why the Caged Bird Sings.

For years I have listened to people during a critical stage of despair, a stage where they've felt life no longer had a meaning and they've been tempted to just end it all. At that point in someone's life, there's no point in trying to hand over some package and say, "Here, believe this" or "Think this" or "Do that" and hope that it'll offer some kind of salvation. Nobody else's package really matters at that instant. And because I don't have a package to sell, what I've offered has been my own companionship in those moments when someone is trying to tolerate no meaning or to tolerate life not seeming to be worth the trouble or to tolerate the sense, as I did at an early age, that "Life isn't for me and it's gonna stretch on a long time and I might be doing myself and everybody a big favor by ending it right now." Sometimes the most valuable thing you can offer is not an answer but your presence, your being there to share the feeling of loneliness, your being there while someone goes on breathing in and out, whether it matters or not. Usually, given enough time, there'll be something that'll click, that'll help that person get out of that frame of mind and move on to something else since that frame of mind never lasts. Maybe it'll be something quite simple: being needed by someone or finding some small pleasure that'll help that person feel he can go on.

Having shared in these moments of loneliness, I come to a sort of conclusion that the answer, if there is one, is tied up with human compassion. That's it. We are here to be there for someone else.

Sally Casper,
suicide prevention volunteer,
is a child abuse counselor.

Right now, living in San Francisco as a gay man, I quite often feel that I'm in the middle of a holocaust. I've lost several hundred people. I can't say they were close friends, but easily several hundred people I know have perished. I walk down the street and I see in a newspaper that a friend has died. Since I'm constantly surrounded by that information, it has a tendency to permeate my consciousness and affect what I believe is the message of life.

I have had experiences in the past few years that have proven to me that we're all part of a greater whole and that the reality of our existence is greater than our five senses can fathom. The divisions and boundaries that we perceive based upon our five senses are, in effect, an illusion. It's my belief that the meaning of life changes from day to day, second to second. I believe we're here to learn that we're part of a creative force—I would go so far as to call that force divine. We're here to learn that we can create a world and that we have a choice in what we create, and that our world, if we choose, can be a heaven or hell.

Thomas E. O'Connor,
AIDS activist and lecturer
who has had AIDS-related complex
for nearly a decade, is the author
of *Living with AIDS: Reaching Out.*

These questions are best left to philosophers to ponder because that is their work and it is why they are here.

As a jazz musician, my music touches the heart, mind, body and spirit. A jazz musician is a unique and undauntable person who always knows why he is here and how important his music is to this planet.

My reason for being here has always been apparent to me. I am here to be The Tenor Saxophonist.

Dexter Gordon,
jazz musician and sometime actor,
helped create the bebop sound.

I am not arrogant enough to assume that I know what the meaning of life is. When I contemplate the fact that the universe goes on forever, it is impossible for me to understand. If I think about the endlessness of time, if I think that when I die everything dies with me since everything is only here because I perceive it through my senses; if I spend too long contemplating what the infinity of the universe means—I could literally go mad. So I block those thoughts out.

We kid ourselves. We kid ourselves to make sense out of things. We have to boil the cosmos down to our own very minute frame of reference or sphere of vision. Then we set ourselves up as God because in our scientific quests we start to understand a few of the mechanisms of the life process.

It's still egocentric, but to condense it down to a tiny microcosm: We're here to biologically reproduce, like cats and dogs and bacteria reproduce. Looked at in this way, the meaning of life, for me, has been to give birth to and to love my children. Now, of course, my babies have grown. So for me, today, the meaning of life is nature. For me, the meaning of life is the wallabies and kangaroos hopping around my house, the spectacular parrots. For me, the meaning of life is the wonder of evolution that produces the most extraordinary mix of species of which there are millions on earth and which we are now rapidly destroying. This rather strange species called man is an evolutionary aberrant intent on destroying nature and, therefore, the meaning of life.

Ah, the smell of flowers. I've just put flowers in a vase. The meaning of life is the flowers in the vase.

Helen Caldicott,
Australian pediatrician and antinuclear proponent, is founding president of Physicians for Social Responsibility.

Whatever the reasons for our being here, surely one of them must be to give us the opportunity to do something, at least in some small way, to make the world a better place. Contrary to the philosophy of Yuppies, I do not believe we can help the world very much simply by helping ourselves. We have to help others. And my "others" include other creatures.

Many years ago, I joined just about every animal society I could find. I even got as far as honorary vice president of the National Catholic Society for Animal Welfare—which is as far as a Boston Episcopalian can go. I was, after all, jeopardizing my own future. I know lately there has been some question about the gender of the Almighty, but I've never heard His or Her Episcopalianism questioned.

Many years ago, too, I had an argument with a Catholic priest about his church's once prevalent teaching that animals have no souls. I told the good father that his church had said he and I were, in the future, going to some wonderful Elysian fields where animals were not allowed. (I also reminded him that though he might not be quite as far up in those fields as I would be, he should remember Episcopalians are very democratic and I would do my best to try to get him a good spot.) But I also said that if he and I were going there, and the animals were not going anywhere, then that was all the more reason to give them a little better shake in the one life they did have.

Heavenly argument aside, I believe animals have just as much nobility of spirit and character as we have, that they have courage and fortitude in the face of far worse hardships and dangers than we have and that, finally, they are capable of even more loyalty and faithfulness and lovingness than we are. I believe, too, that if, as the Bible says, "Into our hands they are delivered," they still are, as we are, God's creatures and that we have been given a test of trust to treat them decently. So far, in almost every way one can imagine, we have failed this test—and, come Judgment Day, I do not believe that even a merciful God will forgive us for what we have done.

Cleveland Amory,
writer and animal rights supporter, is founder and president of the Fund for Animals.

Life on earth is an episode in a story, one that began before we were born. According to our Scriptures, we all lived as spirits with our Heavenly Father before the earth was formed. His purpose, the Scriptures say, was to teach His children to become like Him and to give them eternal life. But in heaven we could not learn all we needed to know, and so we left God and came to earth, where we experience good and evil for ourselves in preparation for returning to live with Him. Whenever Mormons run into suffering, confusion or defeat, they go back to this story to regain perspective. It reminds us that the point of earth-life is to learn to choose the good on our own, amidst temptation, fear and uncertainty, and that God is there to help us through our trials.

Through the inescapable suffering, cruelty and injustice of human life, this story of our spiritual origins seems to enable Mormons to rise above despair. The story teaches us that our very purpose in being here is to meet with evil—and with God's help to overcome it. In my experience, these beliefs make people work hard at doing good, even against unfavorable odds. Mormons have a blithe confidence that by pulling together we can accomplish almost anything. That was how Brigham Young felt when he told the early Mormons that they need not worry about the accusation that they would all go to hell. If we do end up there, he said, we will get organized and turn it into heaven.

Richard Bushman,
Mormon theologian, is a writer and historian.

(Overleaf)
Harry Benson
TOO POOR TO GO ON SCHOOL TRIP,
BOY FISHES THE DAY AFTER
CLASSMATES PERISH IN PLANE CRASH

Life is possessed by everybody from the garden worm up. It exists because the creator of this universe wanted it to exist. He designed it so it would perpetuate itself. The human being was given a mind, the ability to express himself, and has become very, very elevated. But he's also been aggressive. Passions, greed and irrationality, said Edmund Burke, have to be brought under control. If not, there will be a deterioration in society. The aggressiveness that human beings possess is basically essential to the progress we've made, but this aggressiveness has manifested itself in a lot of feuding and a lot of unnecessary killing over the years. As we become more civilized there will be fewer wars, but I don't foresee that we will become civilized enough in the near future to dispense with war as a means of settling conflict.

William Westmoreland,

retired U.S. Army general, commanded
American forces in Vietnam.

Tom Haley
CONFRONTATION BETWEEN
POLICE AND WORKERS, SEOUL

Arthur Tress
Mosque in Agra, India

To look for a purpose in Life outside Life itself amounts to killing Life. Reason is given by Life, not vice versa. Life is prior to meaning. Life does not die, sing the Vedas. Christ came so that we may have Life, say the Gospels. Ah, these terrific Westerners who anguish over questions other cultures ask with more detachment and serenity, who are believers to the marrow even in their desacralized existence! Human life is joyful interrogation. Any answer is blasphemy.

Raimon Panikkar,
Catholic priest and Hindu scholar, writes about the philosophy of religion.

No Creator
No Meaning
Diamond
Mind
Open
Heart
Light
Step

Richard Gere,
stage and screen actor, founded New York's Tibet House.

If anybody thinks he or she knows why we're here, more power to him or her. I myself don't know the answer to the mystery of creation. I never accepted the idea that everybody's going to go to heaven. It seems to me like a fairy tale, invented because people found it hard to contemplate death. It is a great comfort for some people and that's fine.

I often think we're like perennials that bloom. They're wonderful, they die, they come back the next year. We're part of a generation; it blooms, it dies, it's replaced by the next generation—and I find that very, very strengthening. We are part of a whole: plants, animals and humans, each dependent on the others. I believe we as humans have the great challenge of living in harmony with the planet and all its parts. If we achieve that harmony we will have lived up to our fullest potential.

Molly Yard,
feminist activist, is the president of the National Organization for Women.

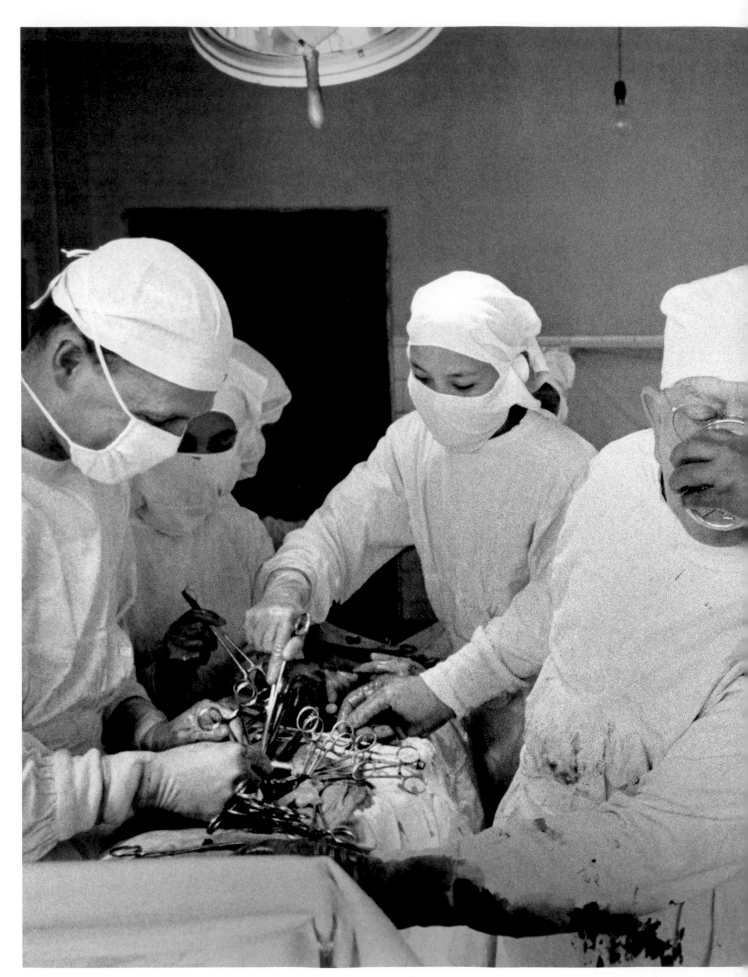

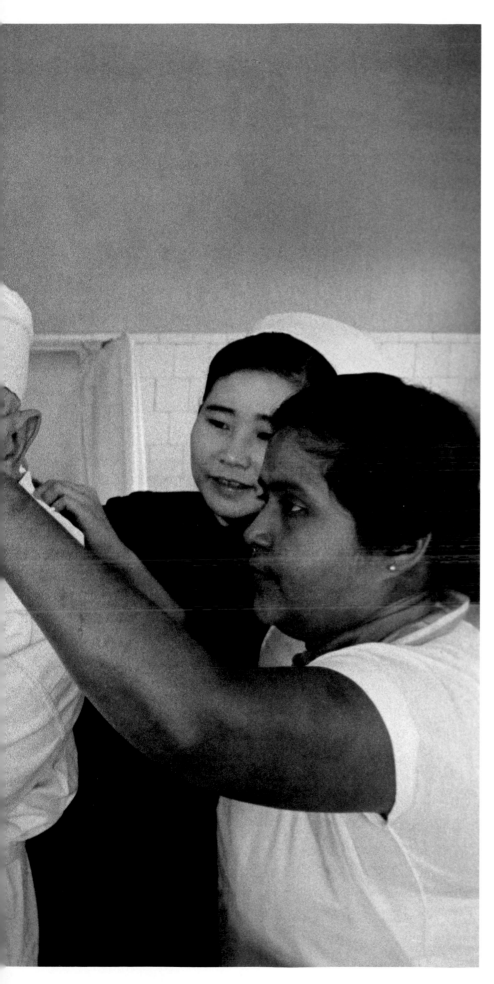

The first thing I look at each morning is a picture of Albert Einstein I keep on the table right beside my bed. The personal inscription reads: "A person first starts to live when he can live outside of himself." In other words, when he can have as much regard for his fellow man as he does for himself. I believe we are here to do good. It is the responsibility of every human being to aspire to do something worthwhile, to make this world a better place than the one he found. Life is a gift, and if we agree to accept it, we must contribute in return. When we fail to contribute, we fail to adequately answer why we are here.

Armand Hammer,

industrialist, physician and
self-made diplomat, was chairman
of Occidental Petroleum.

Larry Burrows
BURMA DOCTOR

(Overleaf)
Fermilab
PARTICLE INTERACTION IN
BUBBLE CHAMBER

The human species has inhabited this planet for only 250,000 years or so—roughly .0015 percent of the history of life, the last inch of the cosmic mile. The world fared perfectly well without us for all but the last moment of earthly time—and this fact makes our appearance look more like an accidental afterthought than the culmination of a prefigured plan.

Moreover, and more important, the pathways that have led to our evolution are quirky, improbable, unrepeatable and utterly unpredictable. Human evolution is not random; it makes sense and can be explained after the fact. But wind back life's tape to the dawn of time and let it play again—and you will never get humans a second time.

We are here because one odd group of fishes had a peculiar fin anatomy that could transform into legs for terrestrial creatures; because comets struck the earth and wiped out dinosaurs, thereby giving mammals a chance not otherwise available (so thank your lucky stars in a literal sense); because the earth never froze entirely during an ice age; because a small and tenuous species, arising in Africa a quarter of a million years ago, has managed, so far, to survive by hook and by crook. We may yearn for a "higher" answer—but none exists. This explanation, though superficially troubling, if not terrifying, is ultimately liberating and exhilarating. We cannot read the meaning of life passively in the facts of nature. We must construct these answers ourselves—from our own wisdom and ethical sense. There is no other way.

Stephen Jay Gould
is a paleontologist, essayist and humanist.

Tui De Roy
LAND IGUANA AND VOLCANIC CALDERA, GALÁPAGOS ISLANDS

(Overleaf)
Alon Reininger
MORNING PRAYER IN
A ZULU PRIMARY SCHOOL,
MAHLABATINI, SOUTH AFRICA

A lot of people talk about love, even though it's almost always mixed up with some other animal/vegetable/mineral traits, even though it's always being conveniently redefined to conform to our clumsy expressions of it. Most people, if pressed, probably could not swear that they absolutely, positively know what it is. Its existence is taken for granted, as if the study of love was not worth the effort of, say, the study of economics or politics.

If we recognize love, it is by its beauty. If we recognize truth, it is by its beauty. The meaning of life is beauty. When we sense and experience beauty, we are looking straight into the face of the creator. We achieve transcendent union with the mind of God. We were born to be aware of it and to create more of it. Money, health, power, comfort mean nothing without it. The beauty of love and truth are what make the ugly parts of life worth enduring.

Todd Rundgren,
songwriter, video artist and
record producer, is founding member
of the rock group Utopia.

Ralph Gibson
Untitled

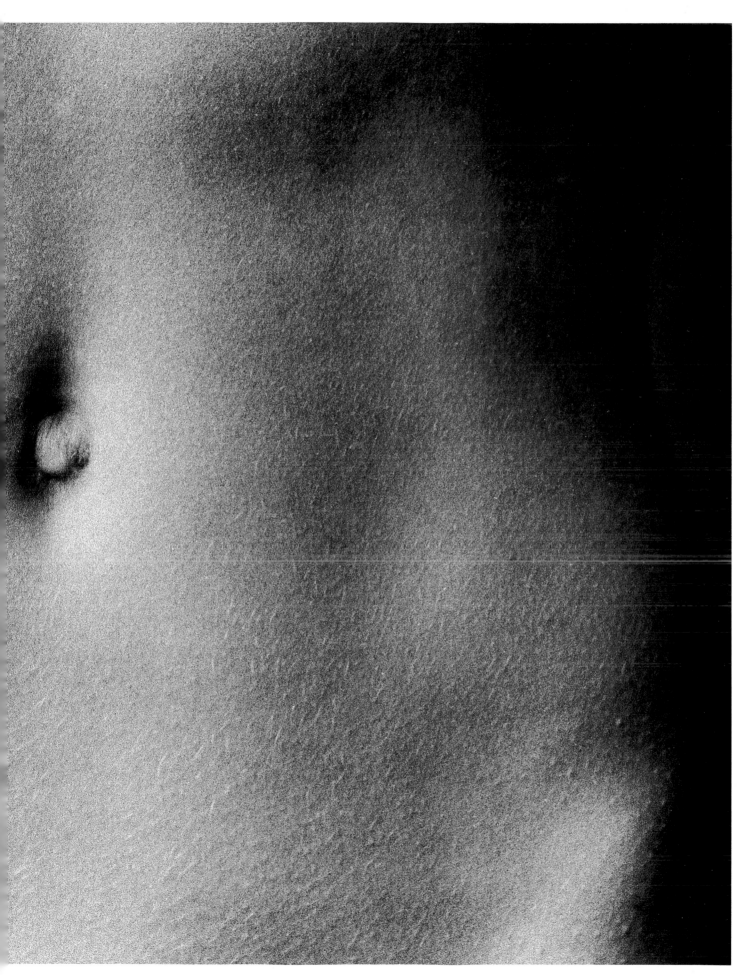

There is no meaning to life. Trying to figure out an answer is beyond us all. People always assume meaning comes through religion, the social structure, the family, work. That's all an excuse for people not being able to cope with the fact that we're here and nobody knows our true purpose. Anybody who tries to apply a direct meaning to life is just grabbing for a security blanket.

Life's destructive forces are authoritarian powers, ruling forces such as government, police, the educational system, the religious system. People were not meant to have power over them. We're meant to have a power within, to run things through ourselves through mutual respect and honor. Too many people abide by laws they don't really believe in, laws they practice through fear instead of sincerity.

I believe in a form of anarchy but it's a misconceived term. It has nothing to do with chaos and violence. It has to do with people leading themselves in a freer form of existence. In true anarchy there is no chaos because there's self-respect and respect for the world. My responsibility is to help evolve our society and our world toward a state in which people want to create a free existence for everybody to mutually enjoy. People don't want to destroy, they want to create.

Amy Keim
is a lead singer in Nausea, an anarcho-punk band.

ABUSE OF POWER COMES AS NO
   SURPRISE
ACTION CAUSES MORE TROUBLE THAN
   THOUGHT
AT TIMES INACTIVITY IS PREFERABLE
   TO MINDLESS FUNCTIONING
CHILDREN ARE THE MOST CRUEL OF
   ALL
CHILDREN ARE THE HOPE OF THE
   FUTURE
DYING SHOULD BE AS EASY AS FALLING
   OFF A LOG
EATING TOO MUCH IS CRIMINAL
EXPIRING FOR LOVE IS BEAUTIFUL BUT
   STUPID
FATHERS OFTEN USE TOO MUCH FORCE
HIDING YOUR MOTIVES IS DESPICABLE
IF YOU AREN'T POLITICAL YOUR
   PERSONAL LIFE SHOULD BE
   EXEMPLARY
LACK OF CHARISMA CAN BE FATAL
MONEY CREATES TASTE
MURDER HAS ITS SEXUAL SIDE
PRIVATE PROPERTY CREATED CRIME
RAISE BOYS AND GIRLS THE SAME WAY
SLIPPING INTO MADNESS IS GOOD
   FOR THE SAKE OF COMPARISON
THE MOST PROFOUND THINGS ARE
   INEXPRESSIBLE
TORTURE IS BARBARIC
YOU ARE A VICTIM OF THE RULES YOU
   LIVE BY
YOU ARE GUILELESS IN YOUR DREAMS

Jenny Holzer,
multimedia artist, is
the U.S. representative
to the 1990 Venice Biennale.

I have been asking why I'm here most of my life. If there's a purpose I don't care anymore. I'm seventy-four. I'm on my way out. Let the young people learn the hard way, like I did. No one ever told me anything.

Frank Donofrio
is a barber.

For those who believe in God, most of the big questions are answered. But for those of us who can't readily accept the God formula, the big answers don't remain stone-written. We adjust to new conditions and discoveries. We are pliable. Love need not be a command or faith a dictum. I am my own God.

We are here to unlearn the teachings of the church, state and our educational system.

We are here to drink beer.

We are here to kill war.

We are here to laugh at the odds and live our lives so well that Death will tremble to take us.

We are here to read these words from all these wise men and women who will tell us that we are here for different reasons and the same reason.

Charles Bukowski,
chronicler and poet of
the down-and-out, wrote the
autobiographical screenplay *Barfly*.

Harry Shunk
LEAP INTO THE VOID

Richard Misrach
SWIMMING POOL

Jim Marshall
HAZARD, KENTUCKY

Philip Jones Griffiths
U.S. TROOPS PATROL SAIGON RUINS,
PASSING VIETNAMESE WOMAN
WITH HER POSSESSIONS

James Nachtwey
TEJUTEPEQUE, EL SALVADOR

When I was eighteen I was in an automobile accident and went through a near-death experience. I was actually taken away from the scene, presumed dead, and it wasn't until I reached the hospital that the doctors revived my heartbeat and brought me back to life. This is the kind of experience that molds people's beliefs. But I have found that most of my conclusions have evolved from observing life since that time. If I've come to know anything, it's that these questions are as unknowable for us as they would be for a tree or for an ant.

Scholars who have studied myth and religion for many years and have connected all of the theories spawned over the ages about life and consciousness and who have taken away the superficial trappings, have come up with the same sensibility. They call it different things. They try to personify it and deal with it in different ways. But everybody seems to dress down the fact that life cannot be explained. The only reason for life is life. There is no why. We are. Life is beyond reason. One might think of life as a large organism, and we are but a small, symbiotic part of it.

It is possible that on a spiritual level we are all connected in a way that continues beyond the comings and goings of various life forms. My best guess is that we share a collective spirit or life force or consciousness that encompasses and goes beyond individual life forms. There's a part of us that connects to other humans, connects to other animals, connects to plants, connects to the planet, connects to the universe. I don't think we can understand it through any kind of verbal, written or intellectual means. But I do believe that *we all know this*, even if it is on a level beyond our normal conscious thoughts.

If we have a meaningful place in this process, it is to try to fit into a healthy, symbiotic relationship with other life forms. Everybody, ultimately, is trying to reach a harmony with the other parts of the life force. And in trying to figure out what life is all about, we ultimately come down to expressions of compassion and love, helping the rest of the life force, caring about others without any conditions or expectations, without expecting to get anything in return. This is expressed in every religion, by every prophet.

George Lucas,
film director and producer,
created cinema's *Star Wars* saga.

Jodi Cobb
LAKE OF THUN, SWITZERLAND

John Brysor
APPOINTMENT CALENDAR

Charles Duke/NASA

Harold Feinstein
Georgina and Rodi

48

While we exist as human beings, we are like tourists on holiday. If we play havoc and cause disturbance, our visit is meaningless. If during our short stay—100 years at most—we live peacefully, help others and, at the very least, refrain from harming or upsetting them, our visit is worthwhile. What is important is to see how we can best lead a meaningful everyday life, how we can bring about peace and harmony in our minds, how we can help contribute to society.

Scientists speak about evolutionary changes and about how the human body can further evolve. Buddhism also describes the natural evolution of the human body. According to Buddhism there are a limitless number of universes. It is we who are dependent on this Great Triple Thousand World System, rather than our affecting its course. In this vastness, can we ever know why we are here? From the Buddhist point of view, our consciousness has the potential to know every object. Because of obstructions we are, at present, unable to know everything. However, by removing these obstructions gradually, it is ultimately possible to know everything.

Those who believe in the theory of rebirth would say that we are here because of our own past actions. It can also be said that the essence of life is the search for happiness and the fulfillment of one's desires. All living beings strive to sustain their lives so that they might achieve happiness. As to why the self, wishing for happiness, came into being, Buddhism answers: This self has existed from beginningless time. It has no end but for it to ultimately achieve full enlightenment.

The Dalai Lama,
winner of the Nobel Peace Prize, is the exiled spiritual leader of Tibetan Buddhism.

Life is the question put to us at birth and our lives are our individual answers, continuously lengthened or rephrased as we live out our days. If there is any meaning to our existence, it rests solely in the act of living out our lives.

The absence of a concrete answer is okay. If we were to wake up one morning to find "Life is . . ." written across the blue sky, then our attempt to get on with this precarious existence would be a lot less interesting, wouldn't it?

Jenna de Rosnay,
model, is a world-champion windsurfer.

Matthew 5:48 says: "Be ye therefore perfect, even as your Father which is in Heaven is perfect." The purpose of life is to reach perfection. The rose starts as a seed or cutting, then grows and prospers with the sunshine and the rain. After a period of time, the perfect rose blossoms. The human experience is much the same, except that the time span is much greater because man, before he can reach this state of perfection, must return again and again through many incarnations in order to conquer all disease, greed, jealousy, anger, hatred and guilt. In order to achieve perfection man must use his imagination to create an image of himself in his mind as a happy, healthy person, perfect in every way. He must pattern himself after the masters of perfection, such as the great master Jesus. Wanting to be perfect is all that is required. I believe that God has a perfect picture in His mind of everyone living together in love, peace and harmony. And since God always gets what He wants, it is not a question of whether man will reach perfection, but when.

Willie Nelson,
singer and songwriter, has been called the king of country music.

Ancient religion and modern science agree: We are here to give praise. Or, to slightly tip the expression, to pay attention. Without us, the physicists who have embraced the anthropic principle tell us, the universe would be unwitnessed, and in a sense not there at all. It exists, incredibly, because of us. This formulation (knowing what we know of the universe's extent) is more incredible, to our sense of things, than the Old Testament situation of a God willing to suffer, coddle, instruct and even (in the Book of Job) to debate men, in order to realize the meager benefit of worship, of praise for His Creation. What we certainly have is our instinctive intellectual curiosity about the universe from the quasars down to the quarks, our delight and wonder at existence itself, and an occasional surge of sheer blind gratitude for being here.

John Updike,
novelist, poet and short-story writer, is the author of *Rabbit, Run.*

If I had been asked why we are here four years ago, just when my daughter was born and I would stand over her as she lay in her little bassinet asleep and just weep uncontrollably because I was beyond happiness or sorrow or any other feeling I had ever known, I would have said that this small child—my child—and all others just like her, was the reason we are here. Just the other day, though, over her objections, I turned off the *Sleeping Beauty* video she was watching so that her father and I could watch the evening news. Half to herself, half to the empty space in front of her, not directly at us at all, and in a plaintive voice, she said, "Now I'm all alone with my boring parents."

If anyone should absolutely, definitely, truthfully find out why we are here, please do not tell me. If I were to really, really know, I feel certain that I should then ask, "Please, may I now leave?"

Jamaica Kincaid,

novelist and short-story writer, often recounts tales of her homeland, Antigua.

Patt Blue
WELFARE MOTHER OF TWELVE
STUDIES TO BECOME A NURSE

(Overleaf)
Don McCullin
TURKISH WOMAN CRYING OVER
HER DEAD HUSBAND, CYPRUS

Every night we turn on the evening news: a nuclear accident in the Soviet Union, an oil spill off Alaska, the destruction of Brazil's rain forests, an ozone hole here, a drought there. And we find it somewhat comforting since the disasters seem to affect strangers in faraway places, as if we weren't, in fact, members of one world. We're like a wildebeest out on the African plains that grazes unconcernedly while lions devour one of our herd.

In fact, we're all connected. If we had the courage, we'd address the fact that this whole technological system that supports our way of life today may also be destroying the planet's natural life-support system. And as a farmer I realize that despite all of the technological advances of the age, my neighbors and I are still at the mercy of the good graces of the same heavens.

We are a spoiled society in the United States. We go to the grocery store and our meals are cut and wrapped, rolled in bread crumbs and ready to pop in the oven. Since we've been blessed with a favorable climatic zone and natural resources, we sometimes think agriculture was created for us alone. We find it difficult to see that food shortages are possible and that there are ways that we can maximize production not to maximize profits or to acquire a bigger share of the world market but in order to feed the world's hungry.

My belief is that a man should be judged not by the duration of his life but by the donation. And our goals should be to contribute something meaningful back to the whole of society, to alleviate world hunger, to make the world a better place for those yet unborn, to build an everlasting peace throughout the world.

Gary Lamb
is a farmer.

Gordon Coster
HARVEST NEAR EAST GRAND FORKS,
MINNESOTA

(Overleaf)
Robert Halmi
MUTUAL CURIOSITY,
AMERICAN BOY AND MASAI GIRL

J. Ross Baughman
Rodeo Hands, Amherst, Ohio

David Turnley
BOLSHOI BALLET, MOSCOW

Larry Siegel
MAN WITH REFLECTOR, TOMB INTERIOR,
LUXOR, EGYPT

Marc Riboud
FAMILY PHOTOGRAPH IN FRONT OF THE
BUDDHA OF KAMAKURA, JAPAN

While calamity jane in a slow
burlesque plays catch in a bone yard
way at the top of a two-legged mare
it was a good night full of bad dreams with
flat champagne and leaves in my hair,
still shooting at birds with a violin bow
first whisper your dreams in your children's
ears making them safe as a hurricane
dangling from a spider web
and across the plate with a swing and a
crack with just a skull for a ball
and a leg-bone bat
and all I remember are sparkle rocks, blue
horses and flamingos as the train begins
to slow and I always saw better when
my eyes were closed

Tom Waits,
performer and songwriter, sings ballads
about the nocturnal, seamy side of life.

Man can be defined as a being
born to transcend himself. And the meaning
of human life resides in man's seeking to
become what he was, is and will be eternally
in God. According to a famous saying of
the Prophet of Islam in which God speaks in
the first person, "I was a hidden treasure
and I wanted to be known. Therefore I
created the world so that I would be
known." Man is the eye through which God
knows Himself in His creation, through
which God sees and reflects upon His own
Splendor. The supreme goal of life is the
attainment of this state of awareness
of being the eye of which God is the light.
This Divine Knowledge also entails love of
God and His whole creation. It requires
correct action based upon His will and
according to ethical principles. As human
beings we have no choice but to accept
the meaning of the precious gift of life for
the use of which we shall be responsible
at the moment of death, that gateway to
eternal life.

Seyyed Hossein Nasr,
native of Iran, is an Islamic scholar.

Why are we here? Throughout
human history the answers to this
eminently practical question have been
limited and defined by the technological and
linguistic levels of the culture.

In the tribal-herdsman culture thoughts
were packaged and communicated in
sounds and gestures. The gods were like
wise, old shepherds with strong voices who
guarded the flock from the ever present
wolves. We humans were here to be
obedient and grateful sheep.

In the feudal-monarchial culture the
"holy instructions" were writ by priests on
illuminated manuscripts.

In the mechanical-factory Gutenberg
culture human beings were here to be
by-the-book—efficient, reliable, productive.
And replaceable.

During the twentieth century a new
scientific philosophy has emerged and
become instantly and universally popular.
It is called quantum physics. The elemental
vocabularies of nature are quanta,
quarks, digital bits of information. They are
writ not in marble or manuscripts or
factory-bound printed pages. Quantum
information ripples, like radio waves
of meaning, across the universe. We are
just now learning to receive digital signals
as they splash over our primitive television
computer screens.

Similarly, the human brain is an array of
one hundred billion digital computers
called neurons. And we now realize that the
brain is obviously designed to receive,
store, process and program these waves of
digital information.

So why are we here?

We are here to decipher the digital
messages from our sponsors.

We are here to learn how the universe is
designed.

We are here to understand the gods who
programmed us.

We are here to accurately emulate their
grandeur.

We are here to learn the language in
which they speak.

Timothy Leary,
American counterculture leader
and psychologist, pioneered experiments
with hallucinogenic drugs.

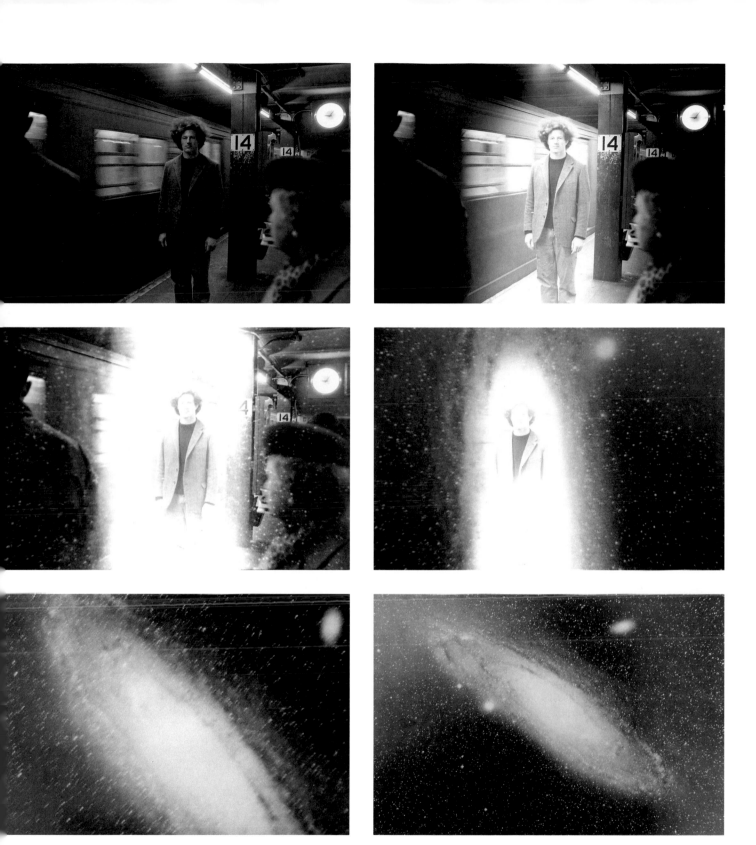

Duane Michals
THE HUMAN CONDITION

I think we're here to make money. You happen to be here and it's your choice to make something from it. It's up to someone's intelligence whether he winds up a derelict on the street or winds up to be a Rockefeller. It's an overused and rotten cliché, but it's on the money: Life is what you make it. I think God throws down people on a planet and says: "Okay. Let's see what you can do. Here's stones and rocks. Here's this nuclear stuff. Let's see if you destroy yourself with it or work something out and make something positive out of life."

When we're born, we each start out as a blank canvas. God provides the paint and brushes. The rest is up to us. We can either make Rembrandts or rejects of ourselves. The lives we draw, the colors we choose—they're all our decision.

Chris DeMatteo
is a mailman.

Why are we here? Perhaps just to ask that question, and to answer it in as many *wrong* ways as possible. First, to take from the world as much as we can, to find out the maximum number of fascinating wrong answers that people all over the world and throughout history have given to that question, to learn their languages and swim in their waters. Then, in return, we are here to give, to make something of our own (the children we raise, the books we write, the people we love), to leave the best fruits of our own courageous mistakes for others to share. Tallulah Bankhead, when asked what she would do if she had her life to live over again, replied, "I would make all the same mistakes, but I would make them sooner." She was right.

Wendy Doniger,
professor of the history of religions, is the author of *Other Peoples' Myths.*

I have always liked the idea that our species is here because some planet-cleaning extraterrestrial beings dumped their troublemakers on a small, empty globe, the way Australia's Botany Bay received its sheep stealers in the 1700s.

If I were still religious, as I was in my youth, I could say that the meaning of life is learning to truly give and receive—between nations, people, species and with our Mother Earth. But having sloughed off religion with a deep sense of relief, coming originally from church-swamped Ulster years ago, I have to admit that I really feel we will be nothing but a short-lived species on the overall scale of things. Honest.

Maggi Peirce,
storyteller, frequently relates tales about her Irish homeland.

You go through life usually doing almost the same thing every day to survive. Some people, they wake up, they don't like what they have to do and it makes the day long. They think about how to get out of doing what they have to do. If you're lucky, you find something that you like to do—and that makes it a pleasure. But when you grow older, have children or grandchildren and look back, you realize for the first time that all along time's been moving. And it's scary.

In the beginning, being a gravedigger bothered me. All you see is the grieving family. You carry the casket. You imagine the person who's in there. And the thing that touches you most is the kids when they pass away. Their caskets are white, for purity, and they're smaller, only like three feet long. They didn't have a chance to experience anything. It's like they were robbed of something. When you see the small white caskets, you appreciate the short, split-second lifetime you have.

Because you don't know what's in front of you, because you don't know if there's life hereafter, you should enjoy it as much as you can while you're here. Go home, hug your kids and thank God they're okay.

Nicholas Vislocky,
former gravedigger, is a cemetery assistant superintendent.

Believe it or not, in all the years I have been on death row I have contemplated very little, if at all, what life means to me. I'm sure that sounds somewhat odd to you considering my circumstances of being on the verge of execution; I am one of the handful of Florida death-row inmates to have survived a fourth death warrant. Living under these present circumstances—being locked in this six-by-nine-foot box, twenty-four hours a day, week after month after year, being totally unable to do as I choose, having no real friends or companions to talk with or share intimate moments—I would have to say, life means very little to me.

In actuality, I have spent more time facing the reality of my execution than contemplating the meaning of my life. For me, my impending execution has more meaning than this daily existence of perpetual punishment. I have reconciled myself to the fact that if I am eventually executed I will be able to handle it mentally. That is, I know I won't break down in tears or fly into hysterics as I'm being strapped into the chair. I must confess I am a complete wimp when it comes to experiencing extreme pain. But I have read numerous accounts regarding people who have been struck by lightning or come in contact with high-tension power lines. In every instance, the survivors related that they never knew what had hit them until they eventually regained consciousness. This realization has made it possible for me to anticipate the worst with a much lessened sense of trepidation and dread. To tell you the truth, I was almost euphoric once that fear was removed from my mind. And by executing me, they will be relieving me of all the daily punishment of my existence. By putting me to death they will, in actuality, be setting me free.

I realize that not everyone shares my disregard for death, but it *is* an attitude to consider. Being an atheist and having no belief in an afterlife or in having to spend eternity in a burning hell has only helped to ease my mind. I won't go so far as to say I am lackadaisical about my impending death, but neither am I paralyzed by fear when I think about it.

Raymond Clark
has been on Florida's death row for twelve years.

In ancient times, the rich hung out at a sort of Republican country club of the day, while the slaves did all the work. While Plato and his friends contemplated the eternal questions, the slaves, unless they were brilliant (patronized tokens like the African playwright Terence), were too busy trying to survive to contemplate such questions as "What is the meaning of life?" For them, staying alive was the meaning of life. The same holds true for most blacks in America today.

Millions of blacks, stalked by unemployment, poverty, violence and death, feel they have no reason to answer the existential questions. Even if you beat the infant mortality odds and you survive the first year of life, you may contract some grave illness; your chances of being treated for it are not as good as those of a white. You may be murdered by another black who knows that his chances of escaping punishment are better than if he had killed a white. Though the wannabe Platos, who make a living at delineating black pathologies, may say that class has superseded race as a factor by which you are judged, you know that if Saint Augustine returned from the grave and showed his black face in one of our fashionable department stores, he would be stalked as surely as any member of the 'underclass.''

Ishmael Reed
is a poet, novelist, essayist and satirist.

I never really thought of why we're here. I guess God got bored.

Michéle August
is an assistant at an Australian modeling agency.

We are here as a result of random occurrences. But what we accomplish since we are here may give some sense of meaning to our existence. Although the notion of "here" can be simply defined as the brief physical time that we exist as individuals, we have the ability to make that "here" extend beyond this physical existence. Man is part of a "collective consciousness." We are connected to one another through time by our creations, works, images, thoughts and writings. We communicate to future generations what we are, what we have been, hopefully influencing for the better what we will become. Our lives are given meaning by our actions— accomplishments made while we are "here" that extend beyond our own time.

Maya Lin,
architect and artist, designed the Vietnam Veterans Memorial Wall in Washington, D.C.

We are very slow learners. We are continuing to destroy Mother Nature. We are involved in wars all over the globe. Each religious group believes it is the one and only one to teach the truth, and these groups persecute, kill and discriminate against all others. In the so-called civilized world, children are physically, sexually and/or emotionally abused; they are the leaders of our future. When children are raised in such a hostile and violent environment, how can we hope for a harmonious future for all the people of this world? We are supposed to be the peacekeepers on this planet, but look what we are doing on a daily basis!

In this light, the purpose of human life is *to achieve our own spiritual evolution*, to get rid of negativity, to establish harmony among our physical, emotional, intellectual and spiritual quadrants, to learn to live in harmony within the family, community, nation, the whole world and all living things, treating all of mankind as brothers and sisters—thus making it finally possible to have peace on earth.

Elisabeth Kübler-Ross,
psychiatrist and author of *On Death and Dying*, is an expert on terminal patient care and society's attitudes toward death.

I used to think that life was all about going to work, nine to five, busting your butt. I was a commodities broker before I was a sock salesman. I worked at Four World Trade Center on the New York Mercantile Exchange. I was a trader. And I lost a whole lot of money in one day. Around fifty thousand dollars. I went from being pretty well-off to being broke—all in one day. After I lost it, I thought, "This is the end of the world." Soon after it was all gone, I realized money wasn't that important anymore.

Then I started selling socks on the street. It has made me a little bit tougher, not as trustful. I have a harder edge to me. Part of the meaning of life is learning that some people come to you with a smile and all of a sudden they're trying to stab you in the back when you turn around. When that happens to me I really don't feel so bad about it because I'm honest, I go to sleep with a clear head every night. I realize that these people who try to "get over" on me—who try to pull a number on me—do not. Life is not about going through the drudgery of work. Life is about trying to enhance your existence: anything from climbing mountains to going up in a hot air balloon to falling in love. Life is more or less trying to surround yourself with good people.

Wayne Silverman
is a sock salesman.

I believe we're here for a reason— created by somebody to live for somebody to return to somebody. I believe that I'm created by God to do the job that He's given me while I'm here, to serve Him and then to return to Him. But it took me a long time to understand this. People pump up professional athletes, saying, "You're the greatest," telling you from day one that you are *it*. Then, all of a sudden, you're not *it* anymore. You're just part of it. Once I stopped playing ball and became an assistant coach in Dallas, I started understanding that I was just a small cog in this big machine. And it sunk in.

Mike Ditka,
former pro football tight end, is head coach of the Chicago Bears.

Brian Lanker
MISS RUBY FORSYTHE, TEACHER I
ONE-ROOM SCHOOLHOUSE FOR 50 YEARS
PAWLEYS ISLAND, SOUTH CAROLIN

ack Birns
AWAHARLAL NEHRU AND FAMILY

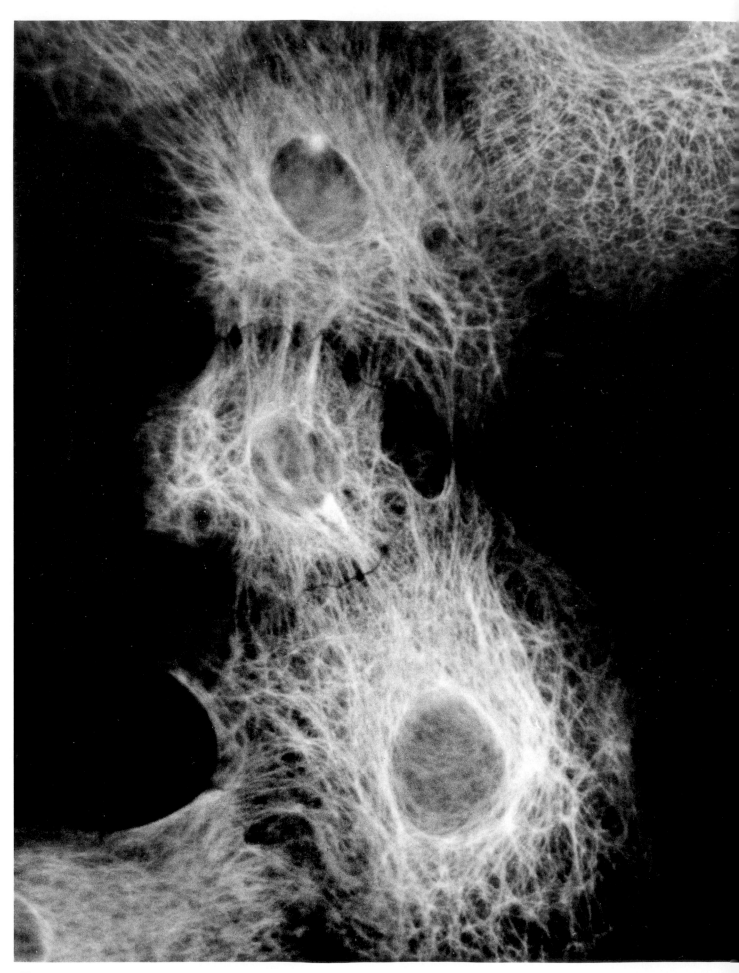

Scouring the windy wastes of eastern Africa in search of the fossilized remains of our ancient ancestors may seem an esoteric and obscure endeavor. However, I deeply believe that our ancestors, who lived, died and were fossilized millions of years ago along the margins of Rift Valley lakes, transmit a special and provocative message to us across aeons of unrecorded time. They tell us that even though we are at the technological pinnacle of life on this planet, biologically we are still susceptible to the whims and caprices of ecological and genetic change. They make us poignantly aware of the great responsibility of the human species as guardian of the natural world. Our ancestors compel us to become more committed to the protection of Mother Earth. It is our duty to respect the natural world that formed us. In doing so, we will assure the survival of man, the introspective species.

I believe that all life is interconnected, intertwined, interdependent in a gigantic web. No matter where we disturb the web, the entire structure vibrates, responds and adjusts. The forces of nature are with us and will always influence the ultimate survival of the species because our existence depends on the blueprint of life, DNA, the same DNA that runs as a thread through all species. I would assert that should life be found elsewhere in the universe, scientists living in that time period will discover that the same principle of natural selection will have been at work.

Donald Johanson,

paleoanthropologist, discovered the skeletal remains of 3.5-million-year-old "Lucy," one of humankind's earliest known ancestors.

Sometimes it is difficult to avoid the conviction that life is just a two-dimensional cinema screen, hung amid blackness and nothingness, upon which a random and meaningless narrative is being enacted. We drift into the narrative briefly and then vanish from it. There is no director or screenwriter or even a projector. But more usually I have intimations of meaning. I know that, as an artist, I make minuscule patterns out of chaos; and by analogy, since the universe is so harmoniously organized, I have to see a mysterious creative impulse behind it. One might as well call this impulse God as anything else.

Darwinists argue that natural selection is a sufficient explanation of organic life. Yet it seems common sense that if an organism moves toward greater complexity, self-consciousness and intelligence, then it is because those qualities are desired. Astronomer Fred Hoyle observed that it was no more likely that our world has evolved out of chaos than that a hurricane, blowing through a junkyard, should create a Boeing.

Looking at certain people who have or had strong religious feeling, I am often impressed by a depth of spirituality that "the good atheist" very rarely has. I am thinking of people like Mother Teresa, Carl Jung, Anna Akhmatova, Boris Pasternak. The last two are great poets; and it is not easy to find poets who have no religious concept. If in doubt, I have always felt, trust the poets.

D. M. Thomas,

British poet and novelist, is the author of *The White Hotel*.

During a period of about a decade, beginning in 1936, my principal research effort was an attack on the problem of the nature of life, which was, I think, successful, in that the experimental studies carried out by my students and me provided very strong evidence that the astonishing specificity characteristic of living organisms, such as an ability to have progeny resembling themselves, is the result of a special interaction between molecules that have mutually complementary structures.

In a world that is not in thermodynamic equilibrium, such as our Earth, parts of which are heated by sunlight, it is possible for certain chemical reactions to be favored, for example by the action of enzymes or other catalysts. A molecule or group of molecules that can catalyze its or their own production is thereby able to prosper. This process, over a period of four billion years, has led to the existence of human beings.

So we are here, in this wonderful world, with its millions of different kinds of molecules and crystals, the mountains, the plains and the oceans, and the millions of species of plants and animals. We have developed a degree of intelligence that permits us to understand and to enjoy the wonders of the world, and also that has given us the power to destroy the world and the human race. With Benjamin Franklin I say, "O, that *moral* Science were in as fair a way of improvement, that men would cease to be wolves to one another, and that human beings would at length learn what they now improperly call *humanity*."

Linus Pauling,

chemist, vitamin expert and advocate of a nuclear weapons test ban, has won Nobel Prizes for peace and for chemistry.

Robert Goldman
MICROGRAPH OF PROTEIN CELLS

Ruth Orkin
"The Wave"
© Ruth Orkin 1981

Abbas
FIREMAN AT SCENE OF BOMB EXPLOSION
BELFAST, NORTHERN IRELAND

This anthology's title reminds me of a justly obscure 1930s book: *100 German Scientists Refute Einstein*. The great man demolished it with a single sentence: "*One* would have been quite sufficient. . . ."

I doubt if this group will be any more successful with *The Meaning of Life*. Indeed, it's a subject where even *one* author may be too many.

The *Oxford English Dictionary*'s first definition of "meaning" is: Purpose. Well, the more we discover about the *real* universe—not the fantasy one of most religions—the less evidence it shows of purpose. (*Design* is another matter; one of the great surprises of contemporary science is how the most intricate patterns can arise spontaneously from complete chaos.)

A wise man once said that all human activity is a form of play. And the highest form of play is the search for Truth, Beauty and Love. What more is needed? Should there be a "meaning" as well, that will be a bonus.

If we waste time looking for life's meaning, we may have no time to *live*—or to play. Our graceful, smiling cousins in the sea may be wiser than us.

"Consider the ant," said the Bible. Good advice, to primitive peoples struggling to survive in a hostile environment.

But perhaps we should consider the dolphin.

Arthur C. Clarke,

British futurist, science fiction
writer and novelist, is the author
of *2001: A Space Odyssey*.

The question is not "Why are we here?" but "How should we live our lives?" The answer is to be found in Aristotle's *Ethics*. All of our technological advances have not changed that essentially difficult question. The Greeks of the fifth century B.C. are our contemporaries; we are no wiser than they were. Remember Harry Truman's response when asked why he was reading Plutarch's *Lives*? Said the President: To find out what's going on in Washington.

Mortimer Adler,

philosopher, writer and educator,
is director of Chicago's Institute
for Philosophical Research.

We belong to nature, we *are nature*; we begin as seeds and decay as weeds. We are born without our consent or desire; we know we are going to die. We spurt out our genes, and leave no other evidence that the fire of individuation spurred us. We travel heads down in the middle of the sky on a grain of confused dust flying among the uncanny myriads. We are peculiarly constructed planetary beasts—freaks, really—designed as limited, repetitive, painfully deteriorating machinery: bellows, lubrication, ingestion, excretion, pincers, pokers, crevices, locomotive waddling.

Why, and to what end? "Yours is not to complete the task, but neither may you leave it off," say the sages of the Talmud. Lenient, benevolent, yet strenuous instruction! A task? What is the task? If we suppose that we are in possession of a task, then it must follow that illumination will not simply befall us, that faith and grace are the easy illusions of nature's dupes, and that there is something *we* must do that nature alone, around us and within us, cannot do on its own.

The task is to set over upon nature, variously through act and interpretation, what naked nature cannot know. Our task is to clothe nature. Our task is to build a shelter in the wilderness. Our task is to devise the technologies of healing. Our task is to impose meaning on being. There is no conscience in nature; our task is to imagine conscience. Nature opposes impediments to its instinct to dominate and devour, and makes us cruel and violent. Our task is the discipline of standing against nature when nature-within-us counsels terrorizing. Our task is to resist evil. Our task is to turn injustice into justice. Our task is to carry a tradition of anti-hatred as strong as instinct itself. Our task is not to spread exculpating lies about the true haters; our task is not to condone hurt through lying. "Whoever is merciful to the cruel," the Talmud reminds us, "will end by being cruel to the innocent."

Our task is to invent civilization. And this is meaning enough to last at least until the snuffing of our local sun.

Cynthia Ozick,

essayist, novelist and short-story
writer, is the author of *The Pagan Rabbi*.

For the past three thousand years our mentality has been going through an astonishing transformation. Before that time, as ancient texts show, human beings were locked into a nonconscious absoluteness, told what to do by hallucinated voices called gods. We possessed what modern psychology calls the bicameral mind: a mind without choice, doubt or wonder. Or even ambition. We lacked even a sense of "selves." It is impossible for us to consciously imagine what it was like. But such a brittle mentality could not withstand the pressures of its own success, such as increased populations, the proliferation of writing and the intermingling of different cultures. In time, the bicameral mind broke down, leaving in its wake the magnificent tapestry of our religions, all referring back to the time when we heard the words of gods.

That mind, over the years, has slowly been replaced by introspective consciousness. This new way of making decisions has left us wishing that we might again feel the continual authorization of divine guidance, and has made us able to ask questions such as "What is the meaning of life?"

This question has no answer except in the history of how it came to be asked. There is no answer because *words* have meaning, not life or persons or the universe itself. And it is in such understanding of all individual selves and all civilizations that our search for certainty can rest. Beyond that, there is only awe.

Julian Jaynes,

psychologist, investigates
the origins of consciousness and
the evolution of behavior.

In the past few decades, the United States and the Soviet Union have accomplished something that—unless we destroy ourselves first—will be remembered a thousand years from now: the first close-up exploration of dozens of other worlds. Together we have found much out there that is magnificent, instructive and of practical value. But we have found no trace, no hint of life. The Earth is an anomaly. In all the solar system, it is, so far as we know, the only inhabited planet.

We humans are one among millions of separate species who live in a world burgeoning, overflowing with life. And yet, most species that ever were are no more. After flourishing for one hundred fifty million years, the dinosaurs became extinct. Every last one. No species is guaranteed its tenure on this planet. And humans, the first beings to devise the means for their own destruction, have been here for only several million years.

We are rare and precious because we are alive, because we can think. We are privileged to influence and perhaps control our future. We have an obligation to fight for life on Earth—not just for ourselves but for all those, humans and others, who came before us and to whom we are beholden, and for all those who, if we are wise enough, will come after. There is no cause more urgent than to strive to eliminate on a global basis the growing threats of nuclear war, environmental catastrophe, economic collapse and mass starvation. These problems were created by humans and can be solved by humans. No social convention, no political system, no economic hypothesis, no religious dogma is more important.

The hard truth seems to be this: We live in a vast and awesome universe in which, daily, suns are made and worlds destroyed, where humanity clings to an obscure clod of rock. The significance of our lives and our fragile realm derives from our own wisdom and courage. *We* are the custodians of life's meaning. We would prefer it to be otherwise, of course, but there is no compelling evidence for a cosmic Parent who will care for us and save us from ourselves. It is up to us.

Carl Sagan,
Pulitzer Prize-winning author and professor of astronomy and space sciences, writes about space exploration and the long-term effects of nuclear war.

There's nothing wrong with thinking there's a next life, a dream-world, a happy hunting-ground, a paradise over the rainbow, salvation. But don't go to church on Sundays to pray to some unknown being who hasn't shown up in thousands of years to come save you. You need to get off your knees and roll up your sleeves and save yourself. Our reason for being here is to have a productive, good, long life and to experience the truth that we're in paradise here right now. In the Old Testament paradise was, at one time, here on this earth. Native American Indians consider earth as paradise. Go into the Adirondacks, assuming you're not in an area where acid rain has killed the trees, go into the Alps, go into the jungle: Paradise is just hanging out, waiting for you. Or go to the United Nations or look at the new stance of the superpowers: I believe that peace is at hand for this planet.

The problem with all the world's religions is that they have commandments engraved in stone, and none speaks about achieving paradise in the 1990s. Christianity had a couple thousand years to try to solve the world's problems, and we're in a bigger mess now than we ever were as we go on killing the planet, destroying our home, devouring the host. How can Christianity address the problems of air pollution and nuclear proliferation and overpopulation when it's geared toward the issues of Jesus Christ's day: the domination of Rome and grinding slavery? Jesus tried to give his contemporaries hope in the next world because he could see there was no hope in the current one.

Why not try what I call ten voluntary initiatives? These aren't commandments; people of this age shouldn't be told to do anything. But they're updated for *today*. And I suggest trying these on for size, as a way of helping foster the idea that our purpose while alive is to make a heaven here. (1) Love and respect the planet and all living things thereon. (2) Treat all persons with dignity, respect and friendliness. (3) Have no more than two children. (4) Help save what is left of our natural world and restore damage where practical. (5) Use as few nonrenewable resources as possible. (6) Use as few toxic chemicals, pesticides and other poisons as possible. (7) Contribute to those less fortunate than yourself to help them become self-sufficient and enjoy the benefits of a decent life. (8) Reject the use of force, military force in particular. (9) Support the total elimination of all nuclear, chemical and biological weapons and, in time, that of all weapons of mass destruction. (10) Support the United Nations.

One way to get this going, believe it or not, is TV. You talk about Marshall McLuhan's idea of TV connecting us all in one "global village." I believe mass communication has helped make us all closer today than we've ever been. And I believe that the gathering and dissemination of worthwhile information to all the peoples of the world is the most important tool we have for achieving the end of realizing that our planet is the address for paradise.

Ted Turner,
cable television pioneer, sports-team owner and yachtsman, is winner of the America's Cup.

Adger Cowan
UNTITLE

Jim Brandenburg
LEAPING WHITE WOLF

National Geographic Society

Why are we here? What is the meaning of life?

These two questions cannot *really* be answered with the mind alone, though intellect can clarify issues and help to point the way. Ultimately, one answers these questions existentially—through a life lived.

Life is given without our input. We live on the dash between our birth date and our death date. The dash does not give us answers, it gives us options and opportunities. Each of us gives a "faith response" and affirmation in every nanosecond of our daily lives as to why we think we are here and what purpose our life has.

Through faith—hopefully on the other side, not just this side, of reason—I believe we are here to do God's will. God's general will is for us to join Him as mortal co-creators in seeking to apply means and ends that are consistent with His nature—which includes love, power and justice—in preserving and making the world, others and ourselves all that it, they and we should and can be.

To fulfill His general will, God's specific will for our individual lives is revealed to us through the gifts He gives us, the context into which we are born, the needs we see around us, our feelings, interests and experiences, our own reason, combined with wise counsel from others, personal prayer and an inner assurance for each of us that this is right.

Each of us has a calling. *Voco*, "to call," is the Latin base of the word vocation. Thus each of us, not just clergy, is called by God to his or her vocation. No one on the giving or receiving end ever seems to regret this truth at the end of his or her life: that the key to life is service to others, service rendered in a way that is liberating and not demeaning. We are not each other's "keepers," we are each other's brothers and sisters. And it is in struggle and service with our brothers and sisters, individually and collectively, that we find the meaning of life.

Jesse Jackson,
Baptist minister, civil rights leader and founder of Chicago's Operation PUSH, campaigned for the Democratic nomination for the U.S. presidency.

I am not a writer, philosopher or Hindu scholar, but a bookkeeper in a urologist's office in Bremerton, Washington. I do not have any profound message as to why we are here, but I think I have a simple explanation all people can relate to. The doctor I work for is on Thanksgiving vacation and I am holding down the fort in his absence. For emergency calls, he gave me the numbers of two alternate physicians. Unfortunately, a number of patients in distress phoned in during the holiday week, and when I called, both doctors were out of town. Eventually, I was able to track down another urologist to get help for these patients. The next day, I called them at home to make sure they had gotten the help they needed. And they were astounded that I had phoned. They told me it was unusual that anyone in a doctor's office would show so much care.

It is not enough to share laughter, art, music, poetry and all the good things in life. We must be there for those in despair. This is the basic rule of this office and the answer to why we are here.

Alma Lyons
is a bookkeeper.

There are persons who apparently view their life span as a mere bookmark between empty pages of darkness. I am not one of them.

To me, every second of life ticks off an instant of triumph, of victory over death and the forces of darkness. Each moment of consciousness is a special grain of time that God has allotted to each of us to make a contribution toward a better world. Through loving we are able to inspire, motivate and uplift others.

As a little girl growing up in Philadelphia, my home was always crowded because my grandmother, Ellen Jane Brown, made her home into a way-station for all of our relatives and friends coming north from Virginia. I never had the luxury of the privacy of my own bedroom. I would always be sharing it with cousin so-and-so. So, as a girl, my idea of a perfect world was to grow up and have my own apartment and be alone—to write the great American novel. Now, with a heaping dose of irony at its best, I've come completely full circle. I now share my home with thousands of kids—poor and misguided, alienated, male, adolescent, predominantly black, most of them gang members at one time. And every day I try to express to these boys the importance of life. Many of them have been accustomed to being prepared not for life, but for death. The high-risk lifestyle of the street has taught them to ignore next month, next year, graduation from school. They concentrate on survival. What I tell them is "Slow down. Live for *this* day. Set goals for next week, then next month, then for life." In time, they begin to realize they *are* going to be around and they *can* include the rest of us in their plans and begin to participate in life. In time, they begin to see that the meaning of life comes in recognizing that they *do* matter, each one of them, and that they are part of the oneness of humanity, sharing a unity with God.

Falaka Fattah
is the founder of Philadelphia's House of UMOJA Boystown, a residential program for troubled youngsters.

Rocco Morabito
KISS OF LIFE

Michael K. Nichol
FIRE HORSE TRANCE, BA

Francis Miller
WORLD SERIES FANS, CHICAGO

Maggie Stebe
WHEN HUNGER OVERCOMES FEAR, HAI

Carl Mydans
Finnish Family in Tammisaari Forest
Cower Under Russian Bombers,
World War II

L ife is a given
of which everyone partakes;
all men, all beasts,
all driven
to one inevitable fate:
to give, ceaselessly,
as the apple tree
its shade, its fruit,
its seed, its root
to other life,
to other beasts,
for other times,
for future feasts.

Chaka Khan,
recording artist, has explored funk,
jazz and rhythm and blues.

John Swannell
UNTITLED

John Domini
DAUGHTER OF BURMA'S PRIME MINISTE
BECOMES BUDDHIST MON

Jeff Jacobson
Winner of Baby Parade,
Ocean City, Maryland

All the wealth on this earth, all the wealth under the earth and all the wealth in the universe is like a mosquito's wing compared to the wealth we will receive in the hereafter. Life on earth is only a preparation for the eternal home, which is far more important than the short pleasures that seduce us here. We have stopped under this tree of life for a short while. We have stopped under a tree of temporary comfort. We have enjoyed its shade. One day life on earth will end and a new world will be resurrected. On that day the entire record of our good and evil deeds will be presented before God for final judgment.

Muhammad Ali,
three-time world heavyweight boxing champion, has been considered the best-known man on earth.

We are not here to predict the future but to change it for the good. We are not here as helpless creatures but as sons and daughters of Adam—capable of affecting our own fate. We are not here to avoid decisions but to make hard choices between good and evil by using an ethical system not invented by man but by our Creator—a framework of truth and moral guidance through which we can find deliverance from despair. We are not here to glorify ourselves, but to glorify He who made us all—and who eventually will judge each of us on how well we did at the end of the journey we all take but once.

Oliver North,
former National Security Council aide to U.S. President Ronald Reagan, was the key figure in the Iran-contra scandal.

In 1988 I was part of a crew of four. We went to Antarctica in a rowboat, crossing the world's "most mad seas." Before we started, most observers deemed it crazy, even impossible. It wasn't. We developed a plan that reduced risk. To me, life is fullest when I try new things. I love that giddy feeling when I bite off more than I can chew, then chew it successfully. That means facing, then dispelling, the fear of the unknown. I want to maximize my potential and, in so doing, inspire others to see through their dreams.

If life is to have meaning, it's essential to carve out your own niche, to become special. Special things happen to special people. Expeditions are not all pure pleasure. Climbing, skiing and ocean voyages to remote corners of the world are often so gnarly and so scary that you wish you'd never left home. But eventually the sun shines again. You must be an optimist. People are adventurous in direct proportion to their shortness of memory.

Ned Gillette,
adventurer and former Olympic skier, has led expeditions on seven continents.

We should ask ourselves this question: Since we are here—and no one asked us if we wanted to be—what should we do about it?

We should make the most of this difficult but extraordinary experience and strive to live in harmony with ourselves and our fellow travelers. We should realize that most unhappiness stems from excessive apprehension and concern about ourselves when we would greatly benefit instead by investing all our thought and effort in confronting far more crucial problems. Most of the human population lives in tremendous misery and starvation, while a small minority enjoys not merely excessive comfort, but luxury. It is my hope that people will realize that it is not through the possession of material goods that one can find happiness in this world. Only by a deep involvement in the problems of the greater society can one achieve happiness or, at least, harmony with oneself.

Rita Levi-Montalcini,
Italian biologist, won a Nobel Prize for her work on cell growth.

The precious gift of life is so fragile that it can be snuffed out in an instant with a single bullet or an error of inches on an interstate. Yet it is so tenacious that it can persist under the most adverse conditions of illness, abuse or privation.

There must be a Giver of this gift, Someone above and beyond our earthly experience. He must have a purpose and a separate mission for each of us that is rational to Him, if not to us, because the mind that created life must have intelligence far beyond ours. As the recipient of the gift of life, each of us should show our gratitude by endeavoring to fulfill our own mission and by respecting all life until the Giver alone pulls the plug. The Donor of life, who designed and carried out so ingenious and intricate a pattern, likewise has a design for His beneficiaries to know Him face to face. It is called everlasting life.

Phyllis Schlafly,
right-to-life activist and attorney, is president of Eagle Forum, a conservative, anti-feminist organization.

Life's meaning is a mystery. I'm not one given to theological musings, but I acknowledge these mysteries. In my own life, the profound root of my being—perhaps coming from my Jewish soul—is an existential imperative that we are here in order to carry forward the human condition not just by having babies but by what we do with our lives. Whatever name we give to God, we sense that there is some purpose in ourselves and we are moved to purposes beyond ourselves. I celebrate my Jewish tradition; in my soul, The Lord, Our God, Is One.

Betty Friedan,
writer, sparked the American feminist movement with *The Feminine Mystique*.

Creation was no accident. God had an intention to breathe life into the world and to make man His masterpiece— so it is written in the Bible.

There is no question that each living creature possesses a divine spark of God; all of us, animals included, are God's creatures. God is life and life is God. Every living creature, as a child of God, is of the highest importance, therefore.

At the same time, I am greatly saddened by the blatant disregard for life I see every day. If man were taught to treat each human being and animal with the love and respect that is accorded to God, the Creator of all things, then perhaps we would not see the shameful neglect of life—murders, wars, slaughters and rapes—that has characterized all of human history. My firm belief is that if we don't respect and love and even worship life, then we don't respect and love God Himself. This is the essence of my religion and the reason for my vegetarianism.

If man could only realize that God created men and animals to enjoy life, not to destroy it, then man most probably would be a lot happier, and the question of why we are here—which is ultimately unanswerable—would not trouble our minds so mightily.

Isaac Bashevis Singer,
Nobel Prize-winning author and storyteller, wrote short stories, novels and children's books.

I think a great deal about the meaning of life, partly because I see so much sexual abuse. It makes you really question why people are put on earth when you witness that kind of suffering. Sometimes I have very bitter thoughts about God being a very bad novelist who's written a terrible draft of a very bad book. And when I hear about something like the discovery of a new galaxy, I think, "Well, maybe that's the revised version and it's better."

At other times—I know it sounds just totally corny—I find myself walking in the park and I look at the way the light falls or I see a tree or sometimes I hear music—Bach—and I think, "Well, this is really fine. So sublime. *This* must be what it's for."

I feel that the purpose of my life is to learn and to feel as much as I possibly can and as deeply as I possibly can and to take whatever it is that I've experienced— the cruelty, the suffering, the beautiful tree in the park—and use it to make something creative.

Andrea Dworkin,
writer and radical feminist, is the author of *Pornography: Men Possessing Women.*

I was born in the South, fifty years after slavery, when racial segregation was legally enforced. I listened to my grandparents talk of their lives as slave children and was aware of the Ku Klux Klan's activity in our community after World War I. Racial pride and self-dignity were emphasized in my family and community because of the seeming insecurities and concerted efforts of many whites to make blacks feel and act inferior to them. I was, therefore, determined to achieve the total freedom that our history lessons taught us we were entitled to, no matter what the sacrifice.

Human beings are set apart from the animals. We have a spiritual self, a physical self and a conscience. Therefore, we can make choices and are responsible for the choices we make. We may choose order and peace, or confusion and chaos. If we choose the former, we may cultivate and share our talents with others. If we choose the latter, we will isolate and segregate others. We can also expand our vision to include the universe and the diversity of its people, or we can remain narrow and shallow and isolate those who are unfamiliar.

To this day I believe we are here on earth to live, grow up and do what we can to make this world a better place for all people to enjoy freedom. Differences of race, nationality or religion should not be used to deny any human being citizenship rights or privileges. Life is to be lived to its fullest so that death is just another chapter. Memories of our lives, our works and our deeds will continue in others.

Rosa Parks
pioneered the U.S. civil rights movement.

(Overleaf)

Michael O'Neill
EARLY MAN

We're here to die, just live and die. I live driving a cab. I do some fishing, take my girl out, pay taxes, do a little reading, then get ready to drop dead. You've got to be strong about it. Life is a big fake. Nobody gives a damn. You're rich or you're poor. You're here, you're gone. You're like the wind. After you're gone, other people will come. It's too late to make it better. Everyone's fed up, can't believe in nothing no more. People have no pride. People have no fear. People aren't scared. People only care about one thing and that's money. We're gonna destroy ourselves, nothing we can do about it. The only cure for the world's illness is nuclear war—wipe everything out and start over. We've become like a cornered animal, fighting for survival. Life is nothing.

José Martinez

is a taxi driver.

Franco Zecchin
SICILY

90

In my first days at grammar school, Sister Agnes introduced me to such truths as 2 + 2 = 4 and the fact that the squiggles on the page were about Dick and Jane watching Spot run (which I knew already from the picture). Sister Agnes was also the school music teacher and she taught us to answer, in cadence and with equal confidence, her question, "Why did God make you?"

God made me to KNOW Him, to LOVE Him,
And to SERVE Him in THIS world,
And to be HAPPY with Him
FOREVER in the next.

She taught such old English rondels as:

Row, row, row your boat	(Confidently)
Gently down the stream,	(Softly. Some kids sang "UP the stream")
Merrily, merrily, merrily, merrily,	(Loudly)
Life is but a dream.	

We all ended up in utter confusion, to everyone's delight, including Sister Agnes. All one could hear was the "merrily, merrily, merrily" part. Over the years, I've come to think that that song was the most important thing she taught me.

Charles Harbutt,
a photographer.

It's really a lot less complicated than we usually think. Life is playfulness. Children know this. That's why they spend so much of their time playing. They are aware of wonder. Adults often need help remembering how to play. We need to play so that we can rediscover the magic all around us.

Looking back, I remember the clouds becoming animals. I remember the moon following me home. There was the time I painted a picture of a sun-shower and was told by my teacher that there was no such thing. What did she know anyway? I had walked barefoot in one. There were countless animals and each one knew how to talk to me. The flowers sang songs that the birds answered. The trees whispered to anyone who would listen. And the rocks both kept and told secrets. They had to be brought home, of course. Every day there was at least one thing to laugh at. Usually there were many.

Hardships help us discover our inner strengths and resources. But we can summon the courage to look at them as opportunities to grow and learn. That's part of life's magic. If we appreciate and respect the children that we were, the spirit of the child within each of us can emerge.

Flora Colao,
social worker, specializes in child-abuse treatment.

In my work I am called upon to make my guests feel welcome and at home. Using a combination of my culinary creations, a pleasant ambience and personal attention, I try to create a special moment, an interlude of warmth and hospitality. It is this sense of the convivial that must be preserved throughout life. It is our duty to give meaning to the life of future generations by sharing our knowledge and experience; by teaching an appreciation of work well done and a respect for nature, the source of all life; by encouraging the young to venture off the beaten path and avoid complacency by challenging their emotions.

Paul Bocuse,
French restaurateur, is the only chef to have received the French Legion of Honor.

The meaning
Of Life
flowers growing you me
taxes birds trees Love
feeling mommy, Daddy,
Bouther, sister, unkl, red, green,
yellow mickey mouse
white, orange, blue,
clows houses man woman
phones John Adams akanomicks
the End

Serin Marshall,
eight-year-old third-grader, plays piano and video games.

Myron H. Davis
BOY AND HIS DOG, IOWA

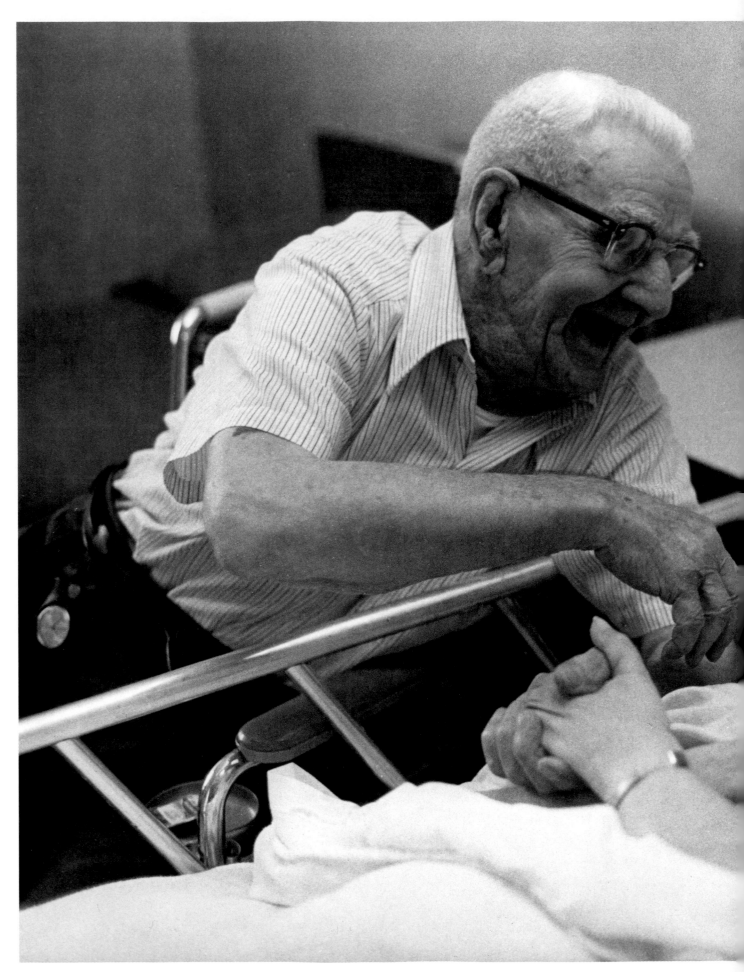

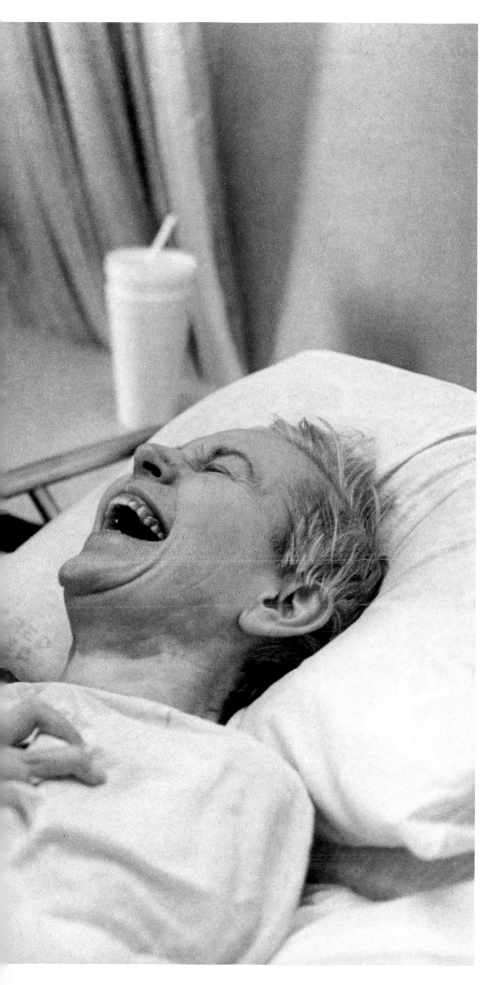

When I faced the loss of my dear grandmother Rose, I asked the question, "Why was she here?" for I could not comprehend a day without her gentle smile and caring touch. The loss was so painful. But as days and months passed, I found that the pain I had felt began to transform itself into something completely new. The empty hole in my life was slowly filled in with a warmth. As I lived again and worked myself into a daily routine, I remembered her words of encouragement. I began to understand that my successes and achievements were her pats on the back, her hugs when I was discouraged and her stories of her dreams and hopes for her children and grandchildren when I had none.

So, the question "Why?" became clear. I realized that my life was an extension of hers. When there is a hole someplace in the world, I believe a warmth eventually fills it. When there is poverty, a richness of spirit eventually comes to help. I believe we are here for each other; to lift, to encourage, to dream. Without that kind of giving, we cease to exist. So, as Rose gave to me, I try to give to others in my work, in my personal life, in my charity. For me, that is why. That is harmony.

Marlee Matlin,
actress, won an Academy Award for her portrayal of a deaf student in *Children of a Lesser God.*

Abraham Menashe
UNTITLED

(Overleaf)
Ralph Crane
"CHICKEN"

95

Bob Adelma
NOT EXACTLY USING YOUR HEA

Susan Meiselas
Freestyle Wrestling Match,
San Salvador, El Salvador

Flying home to Boston from San Francisco on the red-eye, I was aroused from six a.m. torpor by the unexpected sound of laughter and delight. Two rows ahead a toddler was playing a spirited game of peekaboo over the top of the seat with a man in his eighties. Their faces were shining with joy. In no time, a knot of passengers had gathered around, drawn like flowers toward the sun. Tired strangers on a cramped plane had suddenly become fellow travelers on a more enduring journey. We had shared a moment of magic and meaning.

One of my patients told me a similar story that she had forgotten until a severe allergic reaction to penicillin culminated in a near-death experience. She reported floating free of her body and speeding through a dark void into an effulgent brightness that she described as a living consciousness of infinite compassion, love and wisdom. There in the magnificence of the light, scenes of her life replayed. She was amazed that her achievements as a lawyer meant little; the highlight of this "replay" was a chance meeting she'd had years ago with a teenager who had checked out her groceries in the supermarket one day. Sensing sorrow in the boy's eyes, she'd patted his hand and whispered a few words of reassurance. Eyes locked in empathy, they had momentarily forgotten the illusion that they were strangers and shared a moment of deep connection.

We've all had these moments when the heart swells and we feel wordlessly connected to a larger source of loving-kindness and compassion: the times when we surrender to the majesty of a sunset, the caress of a breeze, the laughter of a child, the eyes of a loved one, and we *know* that life is complete just as it is.

Through the ages, people have sought to extend these moments into a lasting state of happiness through practices as diverse as fasting, prayer, meditation, selfless service, psychotherapy, drink and drugs, exercise and laughter. But the core prescription for happiness and meaning handed down through all the world's spiritual teachings is unchanging: *Remember the source with gratitude, and love one another.* In this way the meaning of life as an interconnected web of love and compassion becomes manifest in even the most seemingly mundane moments.

Joan Borysenko
is a cell biologist and psychologist.

All of us experience tremendously moving spiritual moments. The miracle of the birth of a child. A simple sunrise. The breakthrough, after years of struggle, when a nation or a people take to the streets and experience freedom. I've sensed such moments during thousands of hours with my teacher, Rabbi Abraham Heschel: moments of song, moments of silence. I remember walking with Heschel along Manhattan's Riverside Drive one time. He stopped and shouted, "Look! Look!" It was just a sunset. And it was beautiful. And we forgot everything else at that second. We transcended ourselves as we experienced the sun setting.

We live for these moments. Moments of total transcendence are what give meaning to life: when you know you're rising above the humdrum, reaching entirely beyond yourself, realizing that all the words you've been uttering, all the clichés, are real and true. If I may paraphrase the New Testament: In the beginning was the Word. Words, at these moments, take on great meaning. I remember standing in a synagogue in Cairo, reciting prayers. And the first commandment came along: "I am the Lord your God, who took you out of the land of Egypt...." They're words, right? But all of a sudden I felt, "O, my God! I'm in the land of Egypt, thanking God for liberating me from the land of Egypt." Or I was in Selma, Alabama, crossing the Edmund Pettus Bridge, civil rights leader Martin Luther King in front of me. And we burst into song. And at that moment, we felt the power of all the exoduses in human experience over the past four thousand years. We felt connected, in song, to the transcendental, the ineffable. We felt triumph and celebration. We felt that things change for the good and nothing is congealed forever. That was a warming, transcendental, spiritual experience. Meaning and purpose and mission were beyond exact words: meaning *was* the feeling, the song, the moment of overwhelming spiritual fulfillment. We were experiencing what Heschel called the meaning beyond mystery.

Wolfe Kelman
was the executive vice president of the Rabbinical Assembly, the international association of conservative rabbis.

As a medical student and rotating intern at a county hospital, I had the opportunity to deliver babies, assisting mothers who labored and pushed, receiving the babies in my hands. A decade later, I would twice be a woman in labor, and my own babies would emerge out of my own body. These were sacred moments that touched me deeply, that differed from spiritual epiphanies out under the stars (in which I felt myself part of an awesome, patterned and beautiful universe), or those I have experienced in a Christian context (in which I felt the presence of a God who personally loved me). In each of these different, numinous moments, I *knew* that life had meaning; each experience was accompanied by an upwelling of gratitude and humility. These moments, which can be called an experience of the self, or archetype of meaning, are akin to the act of finally seeing the Holy Grail after a long quest. To have an experience is one thing; to have it affect us deeply is another. It is through these moments of grace and gratitude that we acquire a sense of meaning and a desire to live a meaningful life. The personal challenge is how.

Jean Shinoda Bolen,
psychiatrist, is a Jungian analyst.

Grace Robertso
MOTHERS' DAY OF

W**hy are we here?"** is the most profound and important question we can ever ask. The elusive answer cannot be found in the realm of the known or in the acts we've accomplished in our lives. This is because mere survival has always been the surface, bottom-line purpose for our existence. Were survival our reason for being, something within us would grumble: Survival alone does not ennoble us.

Instead, the true meaning—for the corporate mogul, for the homeless man, for the starving child, for the struggling businesswoman—can be found in what we've yet to accomplish, in the realm of the unknown. We must resolve to look deep within, at the unrealized potential of our unevolved selves. Materially, the unknown is one vast nothingness; potentially, it is all things. The unknown within us is where all dreams, thoughts and genius are frozen. The act of searching to make known the unknown triggers the brain. It allows us to incorporate, in ourselves, a greater consciousness, lighting the way for our dreams to enact themselves. Although we seem small in comparison with the whole of the universe, we are equipped with the greatest cosmic hookup ever created: the human brain. The brain—linked unconsciously to the infinite mind where the unknown resides— only facilitates thought, it does not create it. In struggling to find the answer to why we exist, we awaken the infinite mind to the unknown, making known the unknown, bringing meaning to our existence and a commonness to all.

J. Z. Knight

is a spirit channeler.

Charles Harbutt
T**REE FROM** B**ALCONY,** Y**UCATÁN,** M**EXICO**

No earthly purpose satisfies man's longing to find his eternal reason for being. Children grow up, families soon dwindle, financial empires eventually evaporate, jobs are finally completed, life goals are realized and then lose their glitter, a spouse dies, and finally we die, too. finally we die, too.

Is that all there is? No.

Man seeks incessantly for the meaning of life until he discovers the single eternal purpose for his existence. That purpose is the same for every man and woman. God created us because He longs to enter into fellowship with us. We belong to Him by right of creation. We can never know order and harmony in this life until we choose to establish a right relationship with God through His Son, Jesus Christ.

Augustine said, "Thou hast formed us for Thyself, and our hearts are restless till they find rest in Thee."

Our own purpose on this earth is to come into fellowship with God through His Son who died that we might be reconciled to the Father. But the choice is personal and that makes the consequences grave. It means that we determine our own destiny. As much as God desires to be known in the personal daily experiences of men and women, He will force Himself on no one. Man must desire God and seek Him.

Our search for meaning to life will end only when we establish that personal relationship with God and begin our walk with Him—for time and for eternity. Then comes that glorious personal fulfillment described in holy writ as the "peace that passes all understanding."

Jerry Falwell,
Baptist pastor and religious broadcaster, is founder and chairman of Moral Majority.

If we are here by chance—an unplanned biological accident on this planet—then life has no real meaning, there is no cosmic significance to our lives, no inherent right or wrong, no hope for life beyond the grave.

But humanity is not an accident, and life has profound meaning. This is because our Creator, whom we call God, deliberately put us here, and endowed us with a spiritual nature as well as a body and mind. This not only separates us from the animals but also gives us the capacity to know God and to do His will. We discover the true meaning of life only when we turn to God in faith and commitment. Augustine, who spent many years searching for life's meaning, said it well: "You have made us for Yourself, O God, and our hearts are restless until they find their rest in You."

Today we see a confused and bewildered world heading rapidly toward a rendezvous with something that makes us uneasy and often apprehensive. To the Jew, the Christian and the Muslim, we are moving toward a time of reckoning with our Creator. We desperately need forgiveness for our rebellion against Him.

Those of us who are Christians point to an event that staggers our imagination. Christians affirm that God, the all-powerful Creator of the universe, became a man in the person of Jesus Christ. He taught that God is love, and that He is willing to forgive us when we commit our lives to Him. He offered us hope of an eternal heaven.

I believe that He is the answer to every individual's search for meaning.

Billy Graham
is considered the elder statesman of American evangelism.

Why do we ask, "Why are we here?" That is the mystery that may be more than a temporary puzzle despite the infinitesimally brief span each of us has as a person—and all of us have as a species— on this earth. What is the universe doing questioning itself via one of its smallest products? Quite possibly, nothing much. We may be a statistically insignificant happening among a vast range of happenings that just happen. Scientists, mathematicians and philosophers can produce powerfully plausible accounts of why universal happenings should happen to be "us" for a while. They possess an almost divine capacity to comprehend everything and then explain it all away. Hence the attractiveness and rational possibility of the hypothesis, the hope and the faith that we are "in the image of God."

This is not to claim that the universe is made for us (*that* is the essence of sin and idolatry—an idolatry that we are practicing so as to threaten to use up the world and so destroy its beautiful existence and our way of life). It is to believe that we (doubtless among others elsewhere in the universe) have emerged as respondents to the risky creativity, the passionate artistry and the infinite mystery of God.

A central clue to this, a clue to be shared extensively and not promoted exclusively, is Jesus. So we are here to love God and our neighbors as ourselves. We are here to worship and to wonder and to respond to God by joining together in building up the wonderfully worshipful—through love of our neighbors and the cherishing of the earth.

D. E. Jenkins,
Anglican theologian, is the Bishop of Durham.

To know our purpose for being here, we have to know who we are. To know who we are, we have to know God who created us. God's not an impersonal cosmic force. He's not controlling us like robots, removed from His whole creation. He's really personal—in touch with our daily lives. He knows us better than we know ourselves. And as we get to know Him, we come to love and serve Him, thereby getting our bearings for what His specific, individual plan is—His underlying purpose—for each and every one of us. Through knowing God's love, through prayer, we come to find our best self. Each of us has a call. No two of us are alike in our potential for growth and development. Maybe it's the medic in me that envisions a slow and orderly process by which we come to understand our reason for being, by which we renew and become transformed within the ebb and flow of living life with others. Sometimes we find our meaning from our successes. Sometimes suffering is the prelude to understanding, and we realize that eventually, out of darkness, comes light. Hopefully, each person, in time, finds a way of stepping back, climbing to his or her tower to see a panorama of the whole of life, and thereby feels more whole himself or herself.

I chose to try to know God and to find a deeper meaning in life through sharing my life with others, reaching out and being more vulnerable and open to the stranger, the one in need, the depressed and the ill. Part of my map, you might say, was a call to Maryknoll sisters to reach out to others, sometimes during floods, famines and epidemics, serving in Korea, in Africa, the Middle East and Latin America.

Having said this about the specific purpose that each one of us discovers along the way, we do have a common purpose. It is to become part of the life of God; to know, love and serve Him; to come to know and love our brothers and sisters; to be energized and made whole by God's tremendous love for us in this life and the next, a love that binds us all together.

Gilmary Simmons,
pediatrician, is a Maryknoll missionary.

It is basically impossible to answer "Why are we here?"—the question of questions—in postcard size. Yet I do not wish to evade answering.

No human being has ever succeeded in proving rationally that there is a meaning to life—a comprehensive, definitive and absolutely valid meaning. You know yourself the tentative answers: "My family, my work, my career, the enjoyment of life give meaning to my life." But you also know that explaining the meaning of the day is not explaining the meaning of life. The question, then, aims at something more—at the fundamental.

If there really is no First Reality explaining life and the existence of the cosmos, if there is no Inner Reality that upholds us even now and represents the actual mystery of our life, and if there is no Ultimate Reality finally embracing us even after relationships are broken, after activities have failed and plans have died, when depression and illness have driven us to loneliness and despair, then life as a whole is truly *without* meaning.

Yet is it reasonable to suppose that there is no such Most Real Reality? Is it reasonable to say we come from Nowhere and go Nowhere? Surely, no one has any rational proof for this Most Real Reality, which we call God, a word that unfortunately has been abused frequently. Without trust, nothing can be achieved here. This trust need not be irrational and unreasonable but can be a truly reasonable trust: namely, that the dimension of the finite is not everything; that in my life, even now, there is a hidden dimension of the infinite. But it reveals itself to us solely and definitively in death.

I have become convinced that in trusting this Ultimate and First Reality, I am also trusting that there is meaning to my life and death and to those of other human beings—even if this all-embracing meaning, in the face of an appalling amount of foolishness in the world, will often remain hidden. In short, dear friend, I trust, despite everything, that with my life and your life, ultimately something meaningful, good and reasonable is intended.

From this perspective, you might say that *self-realization* is the meaning of life. We are here to realize ourselves in order to become true human beings. But I add from my own experience: My own self-realization must fail if it disregards the self-realization of others. My realization and others' realizations are meaningful only if they are borne and determined by something that is more than we ourselves: Self-Realization rooted in the reality of God Himself. This is promised us by the Judaic-Christian-Islamic tradition. Shouldn't this suffice?

Hans Küng,
Swiss theologian and author censured by the Vatican, is director of the Institute for Ecumenical Research in Tübingen, West Germany.

We are here for communion with God who is Love, the One in whose image and likeness each one of us is made. We find this communion by loving as God loves us.

Love is radical self-giving for the good of another, the denial of self by which our true selves are born. It is the emptying by which we are filled, the foolishness by which we become wise, the weakness by which we become strong. It is the dying through which we come alive for unending life. In this world love always entails sacrifice and suffering, fidelity and forgiveness. It is fulfilled only in death. It is our sole source of joy.

My spiritual father often said that the miracle of all miracles is the ability to transform through love the smallest, seemingly insignificant detail of the routine drudgery of everyday existence into paradise; the ability to become ourselves, at each moment, a fresh paradise to those around us, thereby becoming "gods by grace" for those who are "gods" to us.

Each person accepts or rejects communion with God in his or her own unique manner. For some the way includes an encounter with Christ. For all it includes the encounter with God's Word and Spirit dwelling within us. There are, in any case, no techniques for its accomplishment. The act of communion comes always as grace. For those who know it, it is not life's meaning, purpose or goal. It is life itself: God with us making us what God is.

Thomas Hopko
s a leading Eastern Orthodox theologian and priest.

Life means love. We are here for love. Only love is real and everything is real thanks to love. We are nomads wandering through illusionary space. How to make it real? Only by destroying limits that separate us from others. No violence, no attempts at escape can help, only love.

Too often love is more painful than joyful. The instances of love are much shorter than the periods during which we wait for love to emerge. The meaning of living is mastering the art of waiting.

Georgi Litichevsky
is a Soviet artist.

Lynn Goldsmith
RETIRO PARK, MADRID

Jules Allen
Untitled

Abe Frajndlich
THREE GENERATIONS

There is one world in which we lead one life. For the overwhelming majority of humanity, that life has been short, brutish and intolerable. If paradise were achieved on earth tomorrow, it would be cold comfort for their irretrievable misery.

But there are those who have enlarged the sphere of freedom in the face of these terrible necessities. They are not simply the artists and saints and the great thinkers and doers. They are also craftspeople, trade unionists, rebellious peasants—and clowns and comedians—all of those who do not bow down to what is and to those who assert what should be. Ultimately the dream that we will only approximate is this: that no one shall ever be condemned by his or her birth into a class or race or nation or gender to a life that is less than human; that everyone will choose and shape his or her existence. The good life is led by those who serve this ideal. Our lives are meaningful to the degree that, as individuals or as participants in common action, we make this world the homeland of the human rather than its place of exile.

Michael Harrington,
the late political activist and Socialist commentator, wrote *The Other America*.

We do not "mean" by ourselves; our parents "mean" through us. We are the outcome of our ancestors' attempts at preserving the species.

In the Talmud, Hillel and Shammai argue for years over the question of whether it is better for a person to have been created or never to have been created at all. The verdict? It is better never to have been created, but, having been created, one should examine one's past actions to atone for all evil acts and to prevent such acts in the future.

This laudably stoic and highly moral response to our predicament, however, does not take into account the discomforting absurdity of our having been the means for our predecessors' ends. I'm a fine example. My parents came to the U.S. by escaping the Holocaust of European Jewry. My mother, arriving before World War II, left her parents and four younger brothers, whom she would never hear from again. My father led the nightmarish life of a fugitive, escaping death during repeated forays into wartime Poland. For the rest of his life, he suffered from recurring, terrifying nightmares. Today my emotional life is a duplicate of theirs— without having had the same stimuli. I retain virtually all of their fears, having added a bundle of my own—some of thermonuclear, toxic and millenarian design. The only twist is that I've turned this constant angst inside out and, as the Talmud counsels, I've become a happy-go-lucky doom-and-gloomer. Surrounded by examples of man's capacity for evil, dwarfed by a universe that creates and destroys suns and galaxies in horrific spasms of violence, I end up reduced to a sort of trembling gratitude: The more I expect the worst, the more relieved I am at its not having happened—yet. Consider the joy of not seeing Godzilla when walking along Fifth Avenue.

In short, we are our parents' purposes. We are isomorphs of our procreators in another time and place.

I think it's time to make a baby.

Lester Schwalb
is an urban anthropologist.

There is no "meaning of life" and that's that. We are not here for any purpose. We are not part of God's divine will. We are not here as part of any conscious motivation.

Mankind is one particular kind of programmed robot thrown up by the process of evolution. Like all other species we are dominated by survival-crazy genes. The major difference between us and all the other species of robots is that we have developed a unique capacity for thought and for sophisticated means of communication and the accumulation of knowledge. Evolution has ensured that, as a result, we have come to dominate the planet.

However, this has also meant that we have been able to develop the tools of our own destruction. The first of these is a propensity for greed, rivalry, ambition, bigotry, intolerance and hatred of other members of our species that cannot be conceived by and hence cannot be pursued by the other forms of life. As a result, life is probably not worth living for a large proportion of the world's population. But our survival-crazy genes have imprisoned us in a will to live that prevents most people from making the rational decision to commit suicide.

Sooner or later, however, the decision will no longer be left to individuals. For the second tool of our own destruction is the development of the techniques of mass murder or suicide that have finally reached a point where mankind is likely to be wiped out completely in the not-too-distant future. Thus, in a sense, Nature has overplayed her hand. For the development of our unique capacities has also meant the development of an auto-destruct button that no other model of robot possesses (except, perhaps, an inferior one possessed by lemmings). So the chances of mankind turning out to be more than just a blip in the process of evolution are very small.

Wilfred Beckerman
is a British economist and author.

Ethan Hoffman
BUTOH DANCER

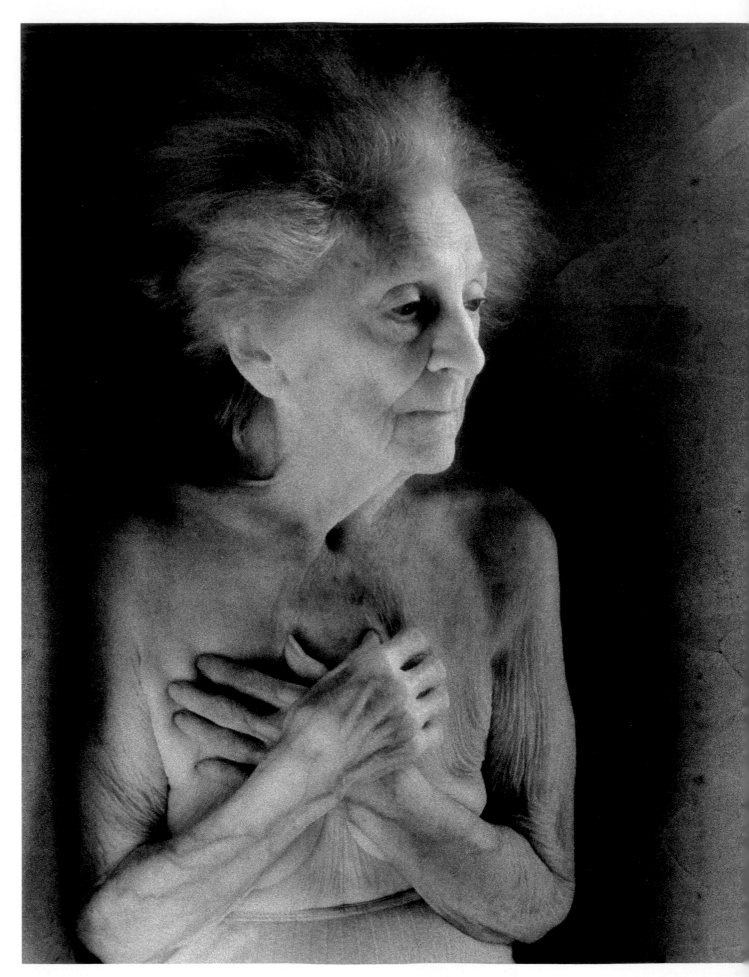

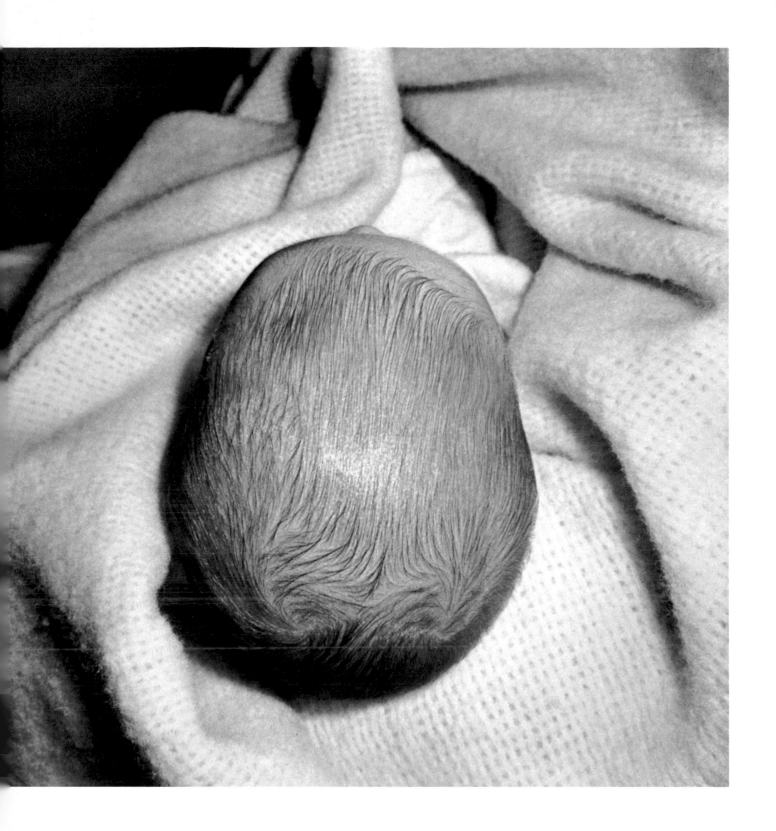

Harry Callahan
UNTITLED

(Overleaf)
**Anonymous/
American Red Cross**
CONCENTRATION CAMP CLEANUP,
AUSCHWITZ

Louise Asher
DOROTHY

You're walking through the forest. There're trees falling down, animal carcasses. Then there's this rusty Coke can. You can barely notice it. Now, is the Coke can nature—or culture? Part of the underlying "why" for our being here comes down to figuring out: What's the deal with this can in the woods? Mankind has some kind of perverse cultural addiction to negating natural processes with our own creations—buildings and computers and bombs. But we've forgotten why we began building them in the first place. We're like the character Arnold Schwarzenegger played in the movie *The Terminator:* a really efficient machine whose motives got lost somewhere. Our purpose is to get back to the reasons behind our creating—the middle ground where the medium and the message are one—back to the human values, the responsibilities to our fellow beings, that first prompted us, passionately, to build these replacement mechanisms. Once we do that we'll have a chance to save the planet so other cats can grow up and dig the forest.

Robert Longo,

post-modern art pioneer,
comments on the urban wasteland in
mixed-media artworks and videos.

My spiritual tradition, that of Wicca, the ancient religion of the Goddess, tells us that the cosmos is a living being and that each of us is a manifestation of that being which constantly reveals itself to us in the cycles of birth, growth, death and regeneration, found in our bodies, in the seasons, in the waxing and waning moon and in all the processes of life. Our purpose is to live in harmony with those cycles, to develop our peculiar organs of consciousness and creativity to add to the beauty, love, humor, diversity and general interest of the world. Our particular challenge in these times is to remake the world so that all people, whatever their race, gender or economic status, have a true opportunity to most fully use our gifts of intelligence, creativity and love. When the balance is broken and the cycles of regeneration are threatened, the meaning of our lives can perhaps best be found in the acts of healing and compassion that can restore the earth and the bonds of human community.

Starhawk,

social activist and writer, is a leader
in the feminist spirituality movement

Why are we here? To take "Life 101," a curriculum of life experiences through which we can awaken into the fullness of our being. Such awakening involves learning how to acknowledge and contain within ourselves the polarities: separateness and unity, life and death, good and evil, activity and passivity, pleasure and pain, and suffering and joy.

Through this process we come to manifest, in our own unique manner, our heart's love and compassion for others, and our mind's clarity and equanimity and power. Thus is Spirit once again manifest truly in form.

Ram Dass,

guru and counterculture figure,
helped form the Seva Foundation.

David Muench
EAGLE CREEK, COLUMBIA RIVER GORGE,
MOUNT HOOD NATIONAL FOREST

Our great purpose in life is to live for the sake of others and to meet the heart of God. However, Western culture is characterized by individualism. This is not necessarily a bad thing because individuality in itself is good. God gave each of us a unique way to serve. But selfish individualism can only build castles on the sands of decay.

Today, a self-centered philosophy and a self-centered way of life lead to the tragic road of self-destruction. To live as Jesus did, totally for the benefit of others, is to find prosperity. This is God's way and this is what Unificationism teaches.

It may seem that such a route would lead to ruin, but it will not. The only reason it may not always bring prosperity is because we do not give to the very end. In that case, the good result never materializes.

When we truly give of ourselves, we are able to meet God. Once the heart of God dwells within us, no matter how lonely we may be, we will be filled with God's love. A person who is completely filled is a joyful person because he lacks nothing.

This true love is also the ideal basis for marriage. Such selfless love allows a husband to live for his wife and a wife to live for her husband. On this basis, they live in unity, harmony and prosperity and give birth to children who grow up in a secure, loving and God-centered family. Such families form the basis of a healthy and peaceful society, nation and world. This is God's ideal.

Sun Myung Moon,
Korean religious leader, is founder of the Unification Church.

We are here to learn to love. Learning to love is terribly demanding and horribly discouraging. Some people never get anywhere with it. And no one ever gets a Ph.D. in the subject.

Children do not start out as lovers. The sun and the planets revolve around them. They celebrate themselves. The snake that spoils their Eden is other people, especially other children. Jean-Paul Sartre once said that hell is other people. But as we learn to love, we find that other people are the channels through which the most profound mystery of the universe—which some of us call God—struggles to reach us.

The most concentrated lesson I have ever learned came to me as I stroked my wife's sweaty hand and rubbed her back one August day during her arduous birthing of our son, Nicholas. That single afternoon in a tiled delivery room taught me more about why we are here than did years of lectures and seminars. The world is designed to teach us to love.

Harvey Cox,
Baptist theologian and divinity professor, is author of The Secular City.

I am here for lunch. Another lunch, really, in my search for the best cappuccino, the best chicken-fried steak and the best flamenco guitar in America. I am not here to be saved, die and go to heaven. I am certainly not here to spend my life polishing my faith. Religion, superstition, faith and belief are the tactics of totalitarians to make me harmless.

Whatever I have to say about greater humanity or universal truth begins with my defense of the basic truths of my immediate universe: the history, art, culture and simple fact of Chinese-American existence. All systems of Chinese thought are systems of personal integrity, not schemes for gutting the soul and perpetuating the state. The Chinaman comes from a civilization founded on history, not mystery. His relationships are martial, founded in Cantonese opera, in arias of tong power, where life is war.

I am here to add to the dignity of human history and to teach my children how to tell the real from the fake.

Frank Chin
is a Chinese-American writer.

I began my voyage around the world when I was eighteen. You don't feel very mortal when you're a teenager. But I became rather intimate with death on several occasions. During a storm in the Mediterranean a wave knocked over my boat, *Varuna*, and filled her up with water. Another time an Arabian cargo freighter passed within a couple of feet of my boat, snagged on the rigging and sliced the forestay. During two and a half years out there at sea I began to feel an omnipresent sense that I could die. At any time. So I now try to live each day, one by one, trying to be decent without excessive anxiety for my future. What do my thirty, fifty or even one hundred years mean in the course of millions that the earth has spent spinning around the sun? Look at how destiny treated the dinosaurs, a group that hardly had a chance to fit in an edgewise word even though they may have had good intentions.

I am here to fit into a minuscule slot of worldly time, to be happy to be alive on a pretty nice planet (to the point of kissing the ground every once in a while), to be able to make some people around me, especially my future children, feel obliged to enjoy life as well. There probably won't be any encores.

Tania Aebi,
adventurer, completed a solo 27,000-mile circumnavigation of the globe in a 26-foot sloop.

There is no grand, overall design to life, no master plan. It's random. After fighting in Vietnam, I don't think I could believe in God again. Having witnessed so much unnecessary death, I cannot still conceive that there is any kind of order. But I do think we find our meaning in life by helping each other and by making better lives for our children.

Kenneth Singleton
is a homicide detective.

Joe McNally
First Dip

What is the meaning of life? Love. To love. To be loved. No surprise there.

Philosopher Max Scheler reminds us, and our experience confirms, that before she is the thinking being or the willing being, the human is *ens amans*—the loving being.

As for God, *faith* impels people to reserve that name for the first and final source of meaning. In the Hebrew Scriptures, faith finds God showing "steadfast love," and in the New Testament, while love is not God, God is love.

I have no good idea and have never met or read anyone who did, as to why evil in the form of hatred exists to counter love. In the drama between love and hatred, however, I find some unfolding of meaning. In communion with nearly two billion fellow humans identified with his name, I find this dramatic unfolding decisively connected with Jesus Christ. I *hope* to learn, in his context, that *love* is stronger than death.

Thus, three italicized words from I Corinthians 13 line up in this game of life: "So *faith, hope, love* abide, these three: but the greatest of these is *love*."

Hence, the meaning of life. Or at least the first hint of a whisper of a clue of finding it.

Martin Marty
is a Lutheran theologian,
author and historian.

The meaning of life is experienced when we are in touch with our unique essence, sometimes called the divine spark within. This spark has no beginning and no end. It cannot be measured in terms of time or space. It is both individual and universal. It is like one light that shines within everything, and yet maintains a distinctive essence within each of us. When we are fully aware of this unique inner radiance, we feel what it is to be utterly alive. We experience unconditional love. We sense complete safety because that spark also connects us to the universal divinity within all things. We feel that all life, within ourselves and others, is precious. We respect, delight in and affirm one another's differences. The more we affirm one another in this way, the more we are capable of greatness.

In this particular lifetime, in this particular period of history, each of us has the opportunity to express our essence through a wholly unique body and personality. The joyous areas of our lives are the areas where this divine spark shines through cleanly, clearly and directly. The areas of pain, confusion and negative emotion are the areas where we are still seeking to express our inner divinity.

The purpose of life, then, is to lovingly accept ourselves and each other, without bias or prejudice, as we learn to unveil the divine spark within.

Barbara Brennan,
former space scientist, is a therapist,
healer and author of *Hands of Light*.

What is life all about? Jesus said it best: "I have come that you may have life and have it more abundantly." How? "Love God with your whole heart, your whole mind and with all of your soul . . . and love your neighbor as yourself. Do this and you shall live."

A more abundant life is a more loving life, a life that loves God, Whom we don't see, as we love our neighbor whom we see all around us, all around the world. Love the Russians? Of course. Love that smelly, ragged old man sprawled on a subway grate for warmth? Certainly. Love the fellow with AIDS? Yes. Love the kid who just mugged you for drug money? Especially.

But really loving them means working for peace, providing for the homeless, finding a cure for AIDS, seeking equal opportunity for minorities—all positive acts of love—pursuing justice, caring and giving of ourselves.

The more abundant life is truly more abundant when we make it available to those who lack it. "What you did for one of these, My *least* brethren, you did it *for Me*." Loving them, you love Me.

Then comes the end of temporal life, and the end turns out to be a beginning of life everlasting. Love comes home where eye has not seen, ear has not heard. And it is unimaginable what God has prepared for those who have loved Him—an endless, new life of peace, love, joy, fulfillment without measure and without end.

Pie in the sky? No, simply faith in God's word which gives life meaning. The alternatives are pretty dreary and hopeless. The meaning of life? There are these three: faith, hope and love, and the greatest of these is love.

Theodore Hesburgh,
Catholic theologian, is president emeritus
of the University of Notre Dame.

(Overleaf)
Burke Uzzle
SKI CHAMPION JILL KINMONT

The human race, which seems to consider itself the crown of creation, is merely one of thousands of living species, all of which are self-evidently products of a long process of evolution from the beginnings of life on this planet. But man is distinguished by the possession of—or possession by—language, which may be a virus from outer space. It is certainly the source of man's endless variety of evil, and indeed the concept of evil is unimaginable without words and without the presence of man on earth.

The human species is in a state of arrested evolution. We are not meant to remain in this primitive physical state any more than a tadpole is meant to remain a tadpole forever. Evolution is a one-way street: For example, when the first primeval aquatic beings moved up onto the land, they left behind their gills and developed air-breathing lungs. Today we can no more imagine the conditions of our future evolution than those fish could imagine life on dry land.

I believe mankind's biological destiny is in space, and dreams are our lifeline to that destiny. It has been shown that preventing a person from dreaming can literally kill him. Who or what has been attempting (with considerable success) to cut off this lifeline to our future? The same forces that have led us to despoil the face of the earth and trample the rights of countless innocent living species. Man, perhaps unfortunately, is not an endangered species; but he endangers all other species and even life itself on this planet.

Why are we here? This is the Space Age, and we are here to go.

William Burroughs,

author of *Naked Lunch*, writes about characters living on the edge of society.

The meaning of my life as an astronaut is in helping to lead humanity out of our earthly cradle to the stars. I see the expansion of our human presence in the universe as a kind of organic growth whose ultimate meaning lies deep in the process itself, as in the development of a seed into a plant. We are following the same urge that drove life from warm lagoons to establish footholds on inhospitable dry land. As we extend human life beyond our home planet, our human consciousness will change.

My most direct experience of space came during the time I spent outside the shuttle, floating in my space suit as a human satellite in earth orbit. As I thought about the deadly vacuum separating my helmet from my gloved hands, I felt the overwhelming hostility that most of the universe has toward life. As I looked down toward my planet, I saw an incredibly thin blue line along the horizon, the earth's atmosphere, the cocoon that shields us from space. Our big, blue sky looks boundless when seen from below, but from above it is frightfully small and tenuous.

In leaving the earth, we are attaining as never before a shared awareness, planetwide, that humanity inhabits a small, fragile habitat in space, a habitat that needs to be cherished and protected. My life is enriched by my being fortunate enough to play a small role in this drama.

Jeffrey Hoffman,

astronaut and astrophysicist, has flown aboard the U.S. space shuttle.

The problem of our purpose is a religious problem. We cannot become enlightened on the subject by peering through microscopes or performing chemical analysis. Our purpose is derived from faith and is imposed onto reality by our own souls. But faith and religious truth themselves are not absolute. They are relative. Thus the answers one gives to questions about the purpose of life must necessarily be relative to a time, a place, a tradition.

To me, the meaning of life is contained in the words of Baha'ullah, who says: "I bear witness, O my God, that Thou hast created me to know Thee and worship Thee." To know and worship God means, in Baha'ullah's words, "to promote the unity of the human race and to foster the spirit of love and fellowship amongst men." Humanity has been "created to carry forward an ever-advancing civilization." What this means is that someday there will be a global society in which humanity will realize its spiritual and moral potential. We are incomplete as we live now, in separate groups, races and nations. Over time, as in the animal kingdom, herds will grow and find other herds. My own vision is that for several hundred years, at least, there will be differences between peoples, divisions based on their cultures. As we evolve, individual aggression will continue as we struggle with our impulses, but warfare—organized social groups fighting each other—will be overcome. And eventually the world will be at peace. Ultimately we will all consider ourselves part of one mankind. There will be variation in outlook—it is not only the Chinese who eat chow mein, not only the Italians who eat pizza—but the variations will not be based on nationality or race or religious differences. The destiny of mankind, actually, is the ultimate creation of a world civilization. It is only in the service of such a cause that I find the meaning and purpose of life.

Firuz Kazemzadeh,

historian, is a member of the U.S. governing body for the Baha'i faith.

Thomas Sanders
Forty-three Parachutists
Somewhere over Illinois

I cannot resist answering this unanswerable question with a memorable statement by William James. Posing the conundrum, "Is life worth living?" he replied: "That depends on the liver." This, I submit, is a profound pun. One's sense of the worthwhileness of life—and, with that, its meaning—owes much to one's health, physical and mental. Indeed, it has been said that someone who needs to ask such questions is already sicklied o'er with the pale cast of thought. And the meaning of life, James suggests further, is a matter for individual decision; all attempts at general statements (including this one) are at best mostly irrelevant and at worst sheer nonsense.

For more centuries and with more energy than I care to think, humans have frantically—or pathetically—tried to establish such universally applicable answers to questions about the meaning of life—and death. That effort is called religion, and while, no doubt, religious communities have supplied their votaries with a soothing or bracing sense of belonging, and meted out comfort in times of trouble, no adult can long rest content with scriptural or theological or pseudo-historical fairy tales. They are of the same order as other anodynes like drink, drugs or seductive entertainment. Individuals must discover the meaning of life themselves. Those whose lives are most meaningful are those who don't need to ask, "Why are we here?" Of course, a stiff drink once in a while is not to be despised.

Peter Gay,
historian and biographer, is the author of *Freud: A Life for Our Time.*

Although religious believers have great differences of opinion, in the final analysis they all come to the same credo: I am here in order to fulfill the designs of the Creator as I understand them and to the best of my ability.

I think that nonbelievers and agnostics in fact are not so far from a similar response to the question of why we exist. Perhaps the most consistent thought of a nonbeliever is: "The question is inappropriate. As a result of a blind game of nature, man lives and dies without purpose, like a tree." However, the obvious ethical point of the question does not disappear even in this model of the world. This question would inevitably be faced by a tree if it could understand that it is blocking someone else's light, since this thought is the first step in having moral choice. Each one of us creates his own picture of the world, tortuously building an ideal in order to try to live in accordance with it. In that sense, there is no difference between a believer and an agnostic, since an ideal is something that, once raised, transcends man. Thus, we are here in order to "hoist our spirit without anchoring it upon anything," as one of the ancient Chinese philosophers said.

We must admit that the foundations are indeed shaky. The ability of the spirit to maintain continuity—the usual consolation of the materialist—falls to pieces if, for example, certain tenets of the evolution of the universe are true. Even if somewhere in a new universe after a new Big Bang, consciousness were to arise anew, it would bear no trace of the summits and chasms reached by our spirit. It is difficult to reconcile oneself to such a world, if it is even possible at all. The question of why we exist makes sense only in spite of such a model of the world. Perhaps man stubbornly builds ideals, "hoisting his spirit," because the religious mode of thinking is peculiar to his nature.

Sergei Kovalyov,
Soviet biologist, human rights activist and member of the Parliament of the Russian republic, was a political prisoner, living in labor camps and in exile in the U.S.S.R. for a decade.

I have a good friend, one of the very best mathematicians, who worked like crazy for eight months to solve a particular problem. His solution was a beautiful, brilliant achievement—it answered an old question and made real progress in this area. Shortly thereafter, a young woman saw a different way to do it—very simply, very elegantly and in a very short time. The guy was crushed. He thought, "What's it all about? What am I doing?" He went to India for six months and came back a changed man. "I now understand," he said to me, "the meaning of life is life itself." When I repeated this observation to a colleague in computer science, he said, "That may be true, but it doesn't give an algorithm!" (An algorithm is a specific, step-by-step procedure for doing something.)

So what matters? Of course, this is a very personal question. For me, I think our purpose here is to keep trying to understand a little more deeply the universe we are all in, to try to take one more step on this unending quest. And to have fun along the way. Why should someone want to run a three-minute mile, juggle nine balls or go to the stars? It's just human nature to reach a little higher, to go a little farther, to focus a little more clearly. I have faith that if each person in the spirit of his or her activity were to move forward a little, we would all be headed in the right direction, even though it might not be obvious to us how it all fits together.

Ronald Graham,
computer expert, is a theoretical mathematician.

From Athens I learn the pursuit of excellence, that whatever is worth doing is worth doing well; from Jerusalem, the joy of the commandments; from both, that persons may leave the world better for having been in it. But Athens's meaning of life is tragic; for Jerusalem, hope overcomes tragedy.

Committed to this heritage, I must also question it. Overpopulation is making life cheap, people superfluous; hope, having died for Jews at Auschwitz, is threatened for all humanity in the nuclear age.

Many respond with a nihilism foreseen by Nietzsche: Life has no meaning; there is but a void; fill it—quickly!—no matter how! After Nietzsche came Nazism. Hitler was largely followed as a way out of the void, as a giver of meaning. What Hitler gave, however, was not meaning but the worst nihilism—ideological fanaticism.

Today the West is permeated by relativism; it is widely thought that there are no standards by which anything can be judged as wrong. This relativism is generally amiable because tolerant, but it becomes nihilistic when omnitolerant. When shocked by evidences of ideological fanaticism, its best response is a retrieval of its heritage in ways fit for the present age.

Hope was wrested from despair when Auschwitz was followed by a return to Jerusalem as idea became reality and the state of Israel was born. Can Athens's quest for excellence be retrieved? Much excellence never gets a start, or is cut off; all is cut off by death. Athens's wisdom may be retrieved by acceptance of the tragic that is part of wisdom; by the view that a life shot through with the tragedy of death is better—more human, more heroic—than a life of meaninglessness, even though pleasurable and comfortable.

Emil Fackenheim
is a Canadian philosopher and theologian.

The real question to ask is: Why am *I* here?

Each of us was placed here for a special purpose. I believe that it is each person's responsibility to determine what he or she can do to make the world a better place—*and then go out and do it.*

We are here to:

Live together peacefully.

Be honest with ourselves and others.

Stand on principle, never yielding to expediency.

Take full responsibility for our actions.

Control our selfish and acquisitive instincts.

Protect and preserve our home—the planet we live on.

Maintain and improve the most efficient unit of government the world has ever known—the strong family unit.

Manage a world driven by rapid change for the benefit of future generations even though an inherent trait of human nature is to resist change.

Be resolute and unflinching in accomplishing the toughest tasks, where the odds of achieving success are against us.

Risk failure.

H. Ross Perot,
billionaire businessman and chairman of Electronic Data Systems, funds conservative causes.

As paleontology has shown, our species is a latecomer to this earth's party. Our invitation was probably accidental. No one seems to know who's giving the party or why. For just this reason, it is all the more remarkable that we have constructed as much meaning as we have.

Before it is over, we must learn how to live as fully as we can while helping others to do so. That there are so many rich ways to do this is the great glory of life. I don't think any more answers than this one are forthcoming, but this answer alone seems a great deal to me. The mere process of dealing with others, outside of the formal systems that otherwise provide meaning, provides awe enough.

Judith Rapoport,
psychiatrist, is chief of the National Institute of Mental Health's child psychiatry branch.

It is perhaps more difficult to answer the question "Why are we here?" than it is to answer "What ought we to do, now that we are here?" The latter, I suppose, has led to the events that constitute the history of man, so far as we know it; to the development of our social structures; to our sense of beauty, however expressed; to the emergence of the world's legal systems; and to our conceptions of morality and all the other factors that enter, or fail to enter, into it—faith, trust, justice, compassion, understanding, peace.

But here we are. Not one of us asked to be here or had very much to do with his arrival. With our finite minds we cannot presume to know if there is a Purpose. We sense, however, the presence of something greater than we can comprehend, a force as yet unknown to us—perhaps ever to be unknown. So we accept our situation, learn from it, and do the best we can, resting on faith, despair or cynicism, depending on the individual. Overriding all this must be an obligation—self-imposed or externally impressed—to do the best one can for others, to relieve suffering and to exercise compassion. We are all in this together, for life is a common, not an individual, endeavor.

Harry Blackmun,
U.S. Supreme Court Justice, wrote the landmark *Roe* v. *Wade* decision legalizing abortion.

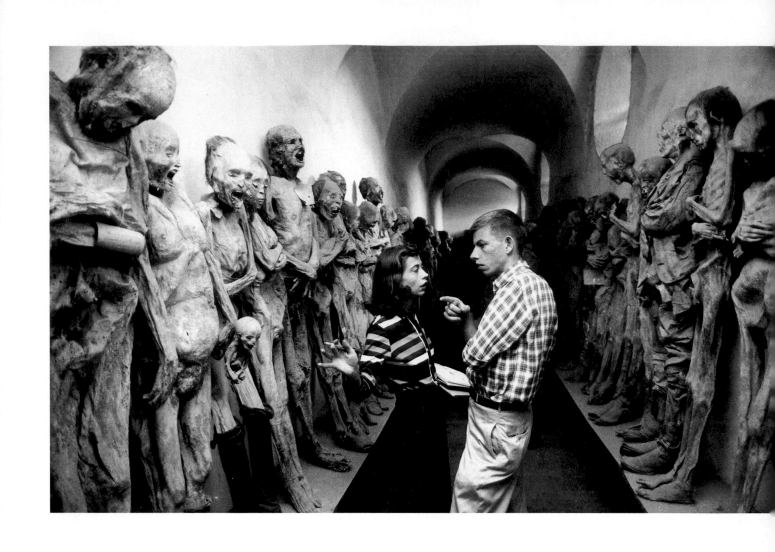

Elliott Erwit
ART STUDENTS IN THE CATACOMBS O
GUANAJUATO, MEXIC

Eugene Richards
The Funeral of Eddie Collins,
Marion, Arkansas

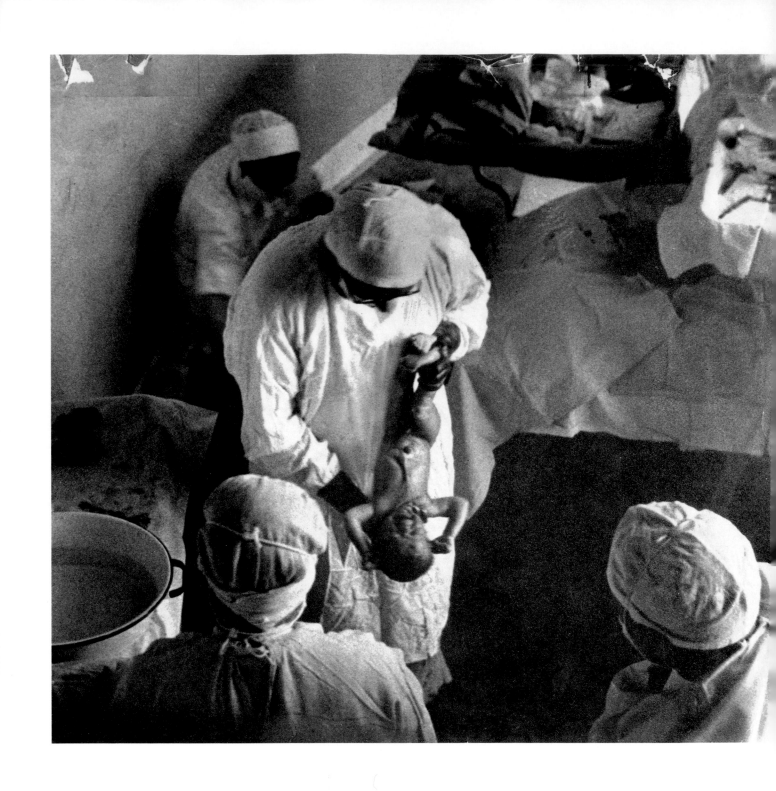

André Da Mian

oyce Tenneson
WO MEN

(Overleaf)
Dmitri Baltermants
ATTACKING THE ENEMY, RUSSIAN FRONT,
WORLD WAR II

131

Joan Lifti
LOWER MANHATTA

I find the meaning of life in a sermon delivered in the third century by a certain Rabbi Simlai. The notes from his talk, part philosophical, part obstetrical, are recorded in the Talmud.

In the womb, a candle burns above the head of the fetus, and by this marvelous light the soon-to-be-person can see "from one end of the world to the other." Furthermore, in those critical months, God teaches the fetus the entire Torah—the whole breadth of Jewish learning.

We enter the world not as strangers to life. We feel at home, we have seen it all before, this thing called life. In the womb, we understand the entire universe and our purpose and the Torah, which provides a sense and set of values. But Torah is for day-to-day living, not for the isolation of the womb. High theory and mere mind-stimulation are secondary; living itself—in the real world, among people—is the essence.

So, at the very moment of birth, an angel slaps the baby over the upper lip, leaving behind that little notch as a reminder. This trauma makes the baby forget the Torah altogether. Next, the newborn has to take an oath: "I hereby promise to attempt to be a *mensh*, a decent, caring human being." Neutrality, noncommitment, indifference have no place in life. To be fully human, we are committed to being caring, sensitive, aggressively compassionate people. Our lives are defined by how we act. We are alive *because* we perform just and righteous deeds, deeds of gentle loving-kindness.

Danny Siegel,

poet and teacher, lectures on Jewish traditions.

L ord Buddha taught us that we are extremely fortunate to have been reborn as humans, having revolved, cyclically, through many possible realms of existence. To have this time and opportunity to seek enlightenment is an extraordinarily precious gift. While alive, we are equipped with a unique kind of consciousness that can choose and make decisions about goals and values. We live in a world where there is a need for loving, compassionate activity; and we are capable of choosing to love and to be compassionate. Our minds are also capable of abstract understanding; therefore, we can choose to pierce the veil of mystery and comprehend the underlying nature of the self and the world around us.

The Buddha also taught us that we experience unhappiness and suffering because of desire, which is a result of the selfishness of clinging to ego. We have the ability to discriminate well enough to follow the direction of those supremely enlightened ones who point us toward happiness and the end of suffering and not to follow the many paths that lead to delusion and meaningless forms of gratification. Therefore, the meaning of life is based on the choices we make, the most profound of which is the choice to practice loving-kindness and joyful concern for the welfare of all beings. The choice to live a life of selflessness is the most profoundly beneficial decision we can make because of its ability to transform our minds and hearts and to bring joy to those around us.

Accepting this greater path of selflessness has the most potent ability to bring about changes in the quality of our lives simply because loving has that power. A life dedicated to selfless activity is a life fully empowered and competent to produce happiness. It is a life unencumbered by the concerns of self-cherishing, and is, therefore, illuminated by the limitless brightness of generosity. Such a life is, itself, the ultimate display of meaning.

Catharine Burroughs,

known as Tulku Ahkön Norbu Lhamo, is the first Western female recognized as a reincarnate Buddhist lama.

U ltimately, our purpose is to be so alive, compassionate and creative in our own lives that the whole universe quivers with excitement and enthusiasm and brings forth a new spirit, a new possibility, in our midst. Our purpose is to be both the womb and the midwife for the birthing into our world of a holy spirit filled with new potentials for life and creativity. We exist in order to quicken the creativity and spirit of our world so that new worlds, new wonders, new blessings may emerge.

The creation of the universe is not finished. It is still emerging. To truly appreciate the meaning of life, we must be prepared to let the meanings we have known stand in the presence of new insights and be transformed. We have no final answers, only the questions that lead to further discoveries, creativity and emergence.

We are here that life may discover, know and express itself more abundantly for the blessing and fulfillment of all creation—past, present and potential.

David Spangler

is a New Age writer, educator and futurist.

Larry Fink
Untitled

Bill Owens
GRADUATION DANCE

Karen Kueh
IDA AND DANNY OF DINOSAUR GARDEN
CABAZON, CALIFORNI

Dolores Metzner
UNTITLED

W̲e are spiritual entities who have created a physical reality in order to add another dimension to our creativity and our pleasure. Living in this physical reality is a great challenge, however, because it is so dense and slow-moving compared with the other levels of consciousness we are used to. For our spirits, it feels like living in a concrete prison, until we learn how to operate successfully here. Once we enter physical reality we tend to become lost in it and we forget the other levels of our existence; we contact those other levels through dreams, maybe through drugs and eventually through meditation and other consciousness work.

Our purpose here is to wake up, to begin to remember the powerful and loving beings that we really are and to learn how to create this physical world as a true expression of the beauty of our spirit. Being in physical reality can add to our joy and freedom rather than diminish it. The physical body is a great sensory organ, allowing us the possibility of experiencing intense pleasure at every moment of our existence. And the human personality allows us to experience great depths of emotion and love. I believe we are in the process of working our way through our fear of simply *feeling too much*, so that we can really start enjoying all of this.

Shakti Gawain,
New Age writer and lecturer, is a leader in the human potential movement.

Joel Meyerowitz
Anawanda Lake

141

Ralph Mors
ALBERT EINSTEIN'S STUD
SHORTLY AFTER HIS DEAT
PRINCETON, NEW JERSE

I believe that man has three basic qualities: a sensitive and intuitive perception that can exercise itself in the world of the senses, an analytical capability that expresses itself in the abstract world of concepts and thought, and finally a prophetic capability that belongs to the artists, the poets, the creators, the inventors.

These three always integrated qualities exist in all human creatures and they are always directed toward the intelligent consciousness of others and of the world that surrounds us. That is why the most natural response to the question "Why are we here?" becomes: to know.

Gae Aulenti,
Italian architect, designed the Musée d'Orsay in Paris.

We are born onto this earth to become enlightened, yet enlightenment is the one thing we are most afraid of. My teachers have shown me that Mother Earth is a schoolhouse of mirrors and that every circumstance and person we encounter is a reflection of our inner need to learn. We are here in a search to find our way home. Home is enlightenment—our inner dwelling with God.

Lynn Andrews,
spiritualist and teacher of shamanism, the author of *Medicine Woman*.

Since the beginning of civilization we have explained our existence in terms of what we could observe. We assumed that the constellations in the heavens above and the beauty of nature on the earth below were there for some purpose. In the hierarchy of medieval times, explanations for man's existence altered significantly. With the beginning of the fifteenth-century European Renaissance, our context changed and the supernatural no longer remained at the center of things. Instead, an era of individual empowerment began. The idea of perspective was introduced into art, and the Cartesian-Newtonian explanation of a well-ordered universe, with us at its epicenter, created the context for understanding that has shaped the next half millennium. What has really changed during this period has been our ability to process information, thanks to the emergence of the printing press and an explosion in literacy. Thus our ability to understand our existence has changed as well, as the spiritual has been superseded by the rational.

Today the amount of information accessible to us is a million times greater than that available to our ancient ancestors. We now know that things exist on a scale that is infinitely large yet also extremely small. Today the most interesting philosophers are the physicists and scientists who are able to observe and describe a theoretical reality of the ultimately large and the ultimately small. They are among the first to see that the context for understanding has changed . . . again. The precision of a mechanical universe no longer explains enough. Once again our curiosity is teased. As our ability to process information expands, new contexts are formed—later to be personalized by artists, poets, scholars and other shapers of society.

What most distinguishes humans from other species is our ability to learn, remember and use abstract information. Between the ages of one and three years, children have an amazing intuitive ability to absorb massive amounts of information that is unequaled at any other time in their lives. It is curious that we seem so unimpressed that a child can simultaneously learn two languages without confusing them at this early age. We think we can teach them our experience and wisdom, yet there is so much more we can learn from them.

In the near future, quantum microelectronics promises to increase information-processing capabilities by a factor of a billion. In less than a century a generation of very young children may be combining their intuitive abilities to observe, discover and massively absorb information with the assistance of personal information technology tools that we as yet can't even imagine. It's likely that we will see a breakthrough in our conclusions about why we exist that will be as extraordinary as the breakthrough experienced during the Renaissance.

Maybe we will discover that the only true reality is a state of mind, shaped by the information we can process and contexts in which we see it. Maybe the Supreme Being we call God can be best appreciated as the power of ultimate understanding. Maybe our destination has always been to learn and grow as we approach the light of ultimate understanding. Only the context and our ability to process information changes.

John Sculley,
chairman and chief executive of Apple Computer Inc., helps promote East-West technological ventures and is chairman of the National Center for Education and the Economy.

भगवान् गोमटेश्वर

LORD GOMATESHWAR

Dilip Meht
JAIN RELIGIOUS FESTIVAL, MYSORE, INDI

144

Josef Koudelka
Costumed Student
On His Way to a Festival,
Olomouc, Czechoslovakia

We are here, charged with the task of completing (one might say creating) ourselves. The process is jazz. It requires improvisation, the daring to strike out on your own coupled with a sure grounding in and respect for the tune on which you are working changes. As Robert Frost says, we must keep the colors of ourselves "unmixed on the palette."

William Cook
is an African and Afro-American studies scholar.

Some modern thinkers would have us believe that a human life is so fragile, so infinitesimal as to be meaningless in a universe dwarfed by a vast and unending cosmic scheme. That is not true. The cosmos teems with meaning. Einstein believed that human experience is fated. And although I believe in some measure of freedom, in the main, I have to agree. Human beings evolve from lifetime to lifetime, and while some experiences may seem inexplicable in the short term of a single lifetime, in the context of the total evolution, no experience is ever wasted or lost. Even the person who seems to be the least important is slowly preparing for some special mission to benefit humankind.

What does this mean philosophically? It means there is a plan. There is a cosmic intelligence, a creator. For despite the artificial barriers men have set up to separate the different formal religions, there is one reality that unites them and reconciles one with another and has equal meaning for all.

Joan Quigley,
celebrity astrologer, advised U.S. First Lady Nancy Reagan on celestial matters.

Life has a definite beginning, but we exist before this, each of us, in the heart and mind of God, Who is not an ethereal being but a personal, eternal being of unmatchable love Who by His very nature operates with deliberate plan and purpose. With a specific set of objectives in mind for us to fulfill, He personally hand-forms each of us in our mother's womb, fashioning us as His own work of art to function successfully within the framework of lifetime activities that He has prepared for us. To discover God's individual plan for us requires that we "fellowship" with Him during our time on this earth. We can get to Him through His son Jesus Christ who died and rose again that we might have eternal life. At death, we will come face-to-face with Him to give an account of how we lived our lives. Having missed His plan is the greatest of tragedies, for it certainly means that we failed to enjoy the satisfaction and success that God had intended for us. Worse, we will find ourselves faced with eternal separation from God for our refusal to come to Him of our own volition. It is only sensible to revere Him and live in His plan and purpose. Since our life, once started, continues without end, it is crucial that we live in such a way that we are able to return to our source.

Elaine Barnes
is a midwife and pediatric nurse practitioner.

There is a Buddhist term, *deai,* that is difficult to translate but perhaps best defined as "encounter." The meaning is more precisely a combination of chance and destiny, of fate with a purpose. I suppose this is my way of summing up how I feel on this question, "Why are we here?" In my own life, where I am often an Easterner in the West or a Westerner in the East, my own feelings reflect a kind of duality of traditions. I think that there is a line that begins before our life here, intersects it and continues after we exist. Chance certainly plays a part in our lives, but it is chance with a purpose.

Seiji Ozawa,
conductor, is the music director of the Boston Symphony Orchestra.

Rock-climbing offers the simplicity of space and silence. While climbing, I'm completely absorbed in the moment, nothing else matters and no other thoughts distract me from fully experiencing life at that instant. The purpose of my existence a I climb is to adapt my personal dimensions to the environment around me at each moment. I become an active player sharing some of the responsibility for my own destiny, achieving a heightened sense of awareness and seeing the direct result of m efforts; either I fall or I reach the top. But meaning does not come from conquering th rock. Purpose comes from moving in harmony with nature, rather than destroying it or altering it for my immedia satisfaction. What gives life meaning is the fulfillment of directing energy in a way that brings a higher order to, and harmony with, the environment I live in.

Though I speak about nature and our environment, the central meaningful feature of our lives is human nature. Life, like climbing, goes beyond ourselves and th rocks. The ultimate meaning of our lives is relative to how much we have given to others. The ultimate meaning of our lives i connected with death. And I know that long after my existence, I would like to hav given something to others that can grow and develop. In short, I would like to know that I have inspired people to go beyond self-limiting stereotypes to experience and nurture the true richness of their passions.

Lynn Hill-Raffa
is considered America's foremost female rock-climber.

Why are we here?" That profound question can be answered in three easy words: TO WORSHIP *ME*. That's right, sex ape, until you surrender your mind, body and candypants to me, Judy, the Petite-Flower, Giver-Goddess, Fashion-Plate, Saint, you will never know the cow-like joy and fulfillment that has heretofore been reserved for members of the Republican party.

The very fact that you are reading this book proves that you are just a spineless squid who can't even cross the street without calling up Big Bird. Well, take heart, trog, you're not alone. Since the beginning of time, when Babs Bush was serving us all up as cream of chromosome soup, every mortal toad and his criminal lawyer brother has been begging to be me. Day and night, videoheads who are still growing gills plead, "O great Giver-Goddess, please tie me up and give my life meaning."

"But how," you whine, "can a low-life swine like me devote my life to you, Judy?" Simple, slug—by joining my religion: JUDYISM. To become indoctrinated into this sacred sect, just follow these simple steps:

1. Drain your brain of all thoughts (or else take up sports).

2. Save all your school lunch money and get plastic surgery to look as much like me as a troll like you possibly can.

3. Burn down your house, rebuild it in the shape of my accordion and erect an altar in the image of my boxer shorts, which will then become the focal point of your existence.

4. Destroy any living thing that does not worship me, be it animal, vegetable and/or critic.

You are now a full-fledged Judy Zombie and are entitled to spend eighteen hours a day selling Madame Judy's Good Luck Sea Cow Pendants on the freeway, for which I will give you in return three cents for food and a kick in the pants.

Judy Tenuta
a comedian.

I've had some bad years. I've played in San Diego. Believe me, I was hoping there was more to life than that. We weren't thinking about the end of the universe. We were just hoping for the end of the season.

Winning and losing is part of our existence but not part of our purpose. Games, baseball games—they're not profound, heck no. Neither is money. In America, you make money, you eat. Grow up in Egypt or an island in Micronesia or someplace with very little water where mere existence—just surviving—is the top priority? Think how important money is. Money? Forget about it.

What's important is this. Already, there are four billion entities like you and me on this planet. Now just look out at the sky. You just can't imagine that this is the only place that has the ability to provide for life. I believe there are other people on other worlds in the universe. There's a macro and micro situation going on here. You're only a small part of a larger process. When you consider the stars you can't even imagine: No end. Infinity. If you can't imagine it—who created it? The awe of infinity probably gives me as much belief as anything else.

In the meantime, what's your purpose on this earth? However you personally view it, I don't believe this is merely a preliminary for a life hereafter. You're put here for an ephemeral period to improve the place. I believe in doing your best to enjoy, experience, provide, create, share, accomplish a lot and make a difference while you're *here*. The choice is yours whether you want to make a big difference or a little difference in your family, in the world, in the entire universe.

David Winfield,
All-Star major league baseball outfielder, has played for the New York Yankees and the California Angels.

Why are we here? There wasn't another place. But we are working on it.

What is the meaning of LIFE? It depends on your subscription.

Robert Rauschenberg,
modern art pioneer, is a painter, sculptor, collagist and printmaker.

Tell the meaning of life in 250 words or less? I burst into laughter at the prospect. What an impossible request! Philosophers have struggled with the question for thousands of years, writing thousands of words. But is it any more difficult to answer an unanswerable question in 250 words than 250,000?

I heard a night doorman remark recently, "It's a short walk from the womb to the tomb." But it's a fascinating walk and we can choose the path with cynicism or hope, destructiveness or creativeness, pessimism or optimism. We can choose to protect ourselves within our own little shells or we can choose to be vulnerable and alive, rejoicing in love and friendship, growing through inevitable pain and grief.

Do our little lives have meaning or are we an accidental skin disease on the face of an unfortunate planet? Are we here for a purpose or is it all nonsense? The only certainty is that we are here, in this moment, in this *now*. It's up to us: to live fully, experiencing each moment, aware, alert and attentive. We are here, each one of us, to write our own story—and what fascinating stories we make!

Madeleine L'Engle,
novelist and children's book author, wrote *A Wrinkle in Time*.

To make a dent.

Studs Terkel
is a Pulitzer Prize-winning oral historian, radio personality and author.

W

hat is the meaning of life? First, let's get straight what "meaning" means. Is it significance, purpose or intention? I like intention, because it's beyond me to ponder the underlying significance of the pure, random fact of our existence. Having faced the idea of chaos, of randomness, I'm free to marvel at the stupefying abundance of patterns, rhythms and interrelations in the little universe I experience. My intention is to do no harm.

Every spiritual discipline calls on its practitioners to *practice* something, some form of prayer, meditation, spinning in circles. I'm not a religious person—too rebellious—but after several million turns of the cranks of my trusty mountain bicycle, I must grudgingly admit a certain awe. A peek at enlightenment. Life flows, and I am borne along in a river of sensation and smells; the faster I go, the more the wind squeezes tears from my eyes. I move and I am deeply moved. All the while, I am on a road. Or negotiating a narrow, tricky path that demands my utmost concentration. I aim for perfection—a fluid, aware state that I never quite reach—though the striving is so sweet!

Never did I dream that the old saw "getting there is half the fun" could inform my entire life. But that is exactly what happened when I decided that almost everything—errands, jobs and visits—could be done on a bicycle. It seems like magic that I've devised a way to earn my keep on two wheels as well. Of course it would be nice to share this knowledge, but in our gas-powered society, self-propelled transportation is heretical. So mum's the word, eh?

Jacquie Phelan

is a world-class mountain bicycle champion.

Co Rentmeester
MY YOUTH

Starn Twin
PLANT #3 DETAI

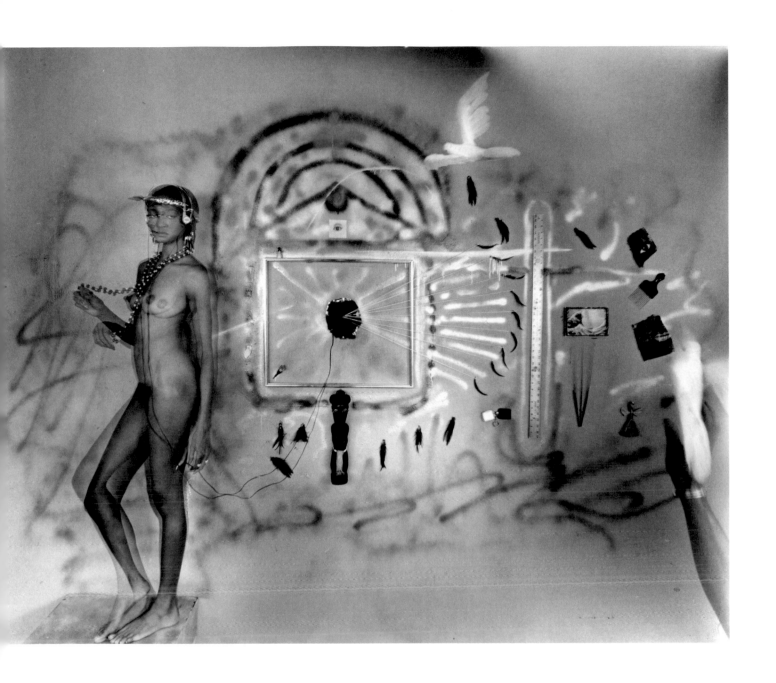

Anthony Barboza
REINCARNATION

God's love is the reason for our creation, a free, gratuitous love, a love without limits. The Lord told us to love each other as the Lord loved us. That is how we should proceed. The message of Christian theology teaches that God loves us all but that God particularly loves the poor. God prefers the poor not because the poor man is good, but because God is good.

Our duty is to translate this love into acts of solidarity and commitment. Two thirds of humanity live in poverty so profound it can only be called death. And the most essential human right is the right to live, a right denied the majority. As humans and as Christians we should express solidarity with the poor and try to change their situation. This does not simply mean on a personal level but by transforming economic and social orders as well.

Gustavo Gutierrez,

Peruvian Catholic priest and social activist, is considered the founder of liberation theology.

David Burnett
MOTHER AND CHILD,
VICTIMS OF DROUGHT,
KOREM CAMP, ETHIOPIA

Enrico Ferorell
JUST MARRIED, MONREALE CATHEDRAL
PALERMO, ITALY

Cindy Sherman
UNTITLED FILM STILL

Courtesy Metro Pictures

Michael O'Brie
PRISON WATER TRUC
HUNTSVILLE, TEXA

W. Eugene Smith
Burned U.S. Officer
in Philippine Church
Converted into Hospital,
World War II

(Overleaf)
Cornell Capa
Generation Gap

T he reason we are here is to ask "Why are we here?" and have the question go unanswered.

Marc Kravitz,
advertising executive and humorist,
is an interactive media expert.

Mary Ellen Mark
CHINA

Ernesto Baza
Untitled, Peshawar, Pakista

162

Bruce Davidson
Ninety-two-year-old Widow in a
Montmartre Park, Paris

I am that I am," said the God of Abraham. Only some such divine tautology would seem to do justice to us all: the old woman who sees ultimate meaning in her grandchild, the mathematician who sees it in a formula, the tribesman who sees it in a crocodile. The meaning of life is that it should mean.

At everyday levels surely meaning is one with nourishment. Clean air, uncontaminated food and water for the body, ideas that exercise the mind and spirit—without these what on earth is meaningful? In our time meaning is threatened at every turn. Nuclear waste, deforestation, greed, plague. God accordingly may be said (by those who still "believe") to have exchanged the mask of creator and judge for that of the firefighter and the paramedic. I put "believe" in quotes because our beautiful human feelings aren't to be trusted. As a poet I know how words, even those words brought together under laboratory conditions, breed meanings not intended by the author. The resulting surprise needn't always be a nasty one. The planet blackened by us as never before may of its own accord break into leaf tomorrow. But this is a mere literary man's daydream, and under no circumstances are the world's lawmakers and corporate heads entitled to share it.

James Merrill,

poet, won the Pulitzer Prize
for *Divine Comedies.*

Hiroji Kubota
Fishing with Cormorants,
Guilin, China

(Overleaf)
Sebastião Salgado
In the Gold Mine of
Serra Pelada, Brazil

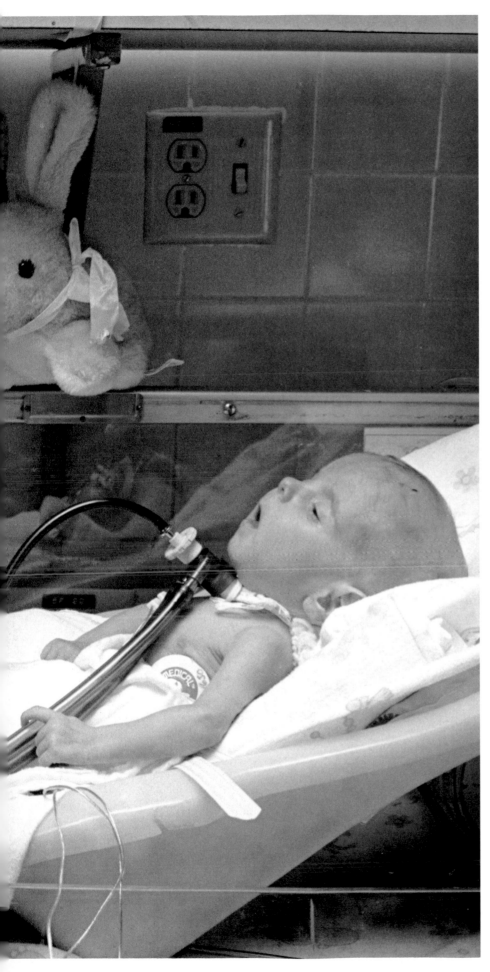

Why are we born was a really hard paper to write. At first for a long time I couldn't think of anything but now I think I no something to say. I think God made us each born for a different reason. He doesn't want us to do the same things so that's why he makes us all so different. If God gives you a great voice maybe he wants you to sing. Or else if God wants you to be a farmer he might give you to a family that lives on a farm so you get used to the animals and your not afraid of them. And maybe if God makes you grow to be 7 feet tall maybe he wants you to play for the Lakers or the Celtics.

When my friend Kim died from her cansur I asked my Mom if God was going to make Kim die when she was only 6 why did he make her born at all. But my Mom said even thogh she was only 6 she changed people's lifes. What that means is like her brother or sister could be the siontist that discovers the cure for cansur and they decided to do that because of Kim. And like me too. I used to wonder why did God pick on me and give me cansur. Maybe it was because he wanted me to be a dr. who takes care of kids with cansur so when they say "Dr Jason, Sometimes I get so scared I'm going to die" or "you don't know how weird it is to be the only bald kid in your whole school" I can say "Oh yes I do. When I was a little boy I had cansur too. And look at all my hair now. Someday your hair will grow back too."

Jason Gaes,
twelve-year-old cancer victim, wrote
My Book for Kids with Cansur.

David Hurn
NINE-MONTH-OLD CHILD IN WARD FOR
PREMATURE BABIES

169

Robert Capa
Italian Soldier Straggles Behind
Column of Captured Comrades
Marching to POW Camp, Sicily,
World War II

Eli Reed
ENELL GETER AND HIS BRIDE,
OUTH CAROLINA

(Overleaf)
David Seymour
FIRST ISRAELI-BORN CHILD IN AN
EARLY SETTLEMENT OF ITALIAN JEWS

171

What are we here *not* to do?

We are poisoning the air, the water and the soil, and we are poisoning our soul. The neutron bomb, which respects things and annihilates people, is the most perfect symbol of our topsy-turvy life. People owe obedience to things, as the poor owe obedience to the rich, civilians to the military, blacks to whites and women to men. To maintain order, this order of the upside-down world, the giant machine of fear manufactures armaments at a rhythm of $2,000 a second, while the media discommunicates us and the educational system diseducates us. One lives to possess, not to be. Money is freer than people. For most of humanity—inhabitants of the third world and the world's slums—the world more resembles a concentration camp than a house for everyone.

This isn't what the world wanted to be when the world still was not. I think that fighting to change it, to recuperate it, gives sense to the human adventure. In this fight I recognize myself in others. In this fight I become a compatriot and contemporary of those who are moved to action by the will for justice and the will for beauty. I am their compatriot though they were born in another country. I am their contemporary though they lived in another age. And thus I feel and know that I am a breeze of a wind that will continue to be when I am no longer— something more than a speck of dust lost in the universe, more than a little moment lost in time.

Eduardo Galeano,
Uruguayan novelist, historian and political activist, writes about Latin American society.

In the winter of 1986-87 I was working as a war surgeon in a Palestinian refugee camp in Lebanon and was facing the prospect that I was going to be slaughtered together with Ben, the man I loved, and the population of the camp. The camp had been surrounded and bombed by a Lebanese militia, and after four months of siege our food had run out and we were beginning to starve. I was thirty-five years old and I did not want to die.

During those hungry days, between operations and often sitting in the dark, I thought over the meaning of life and death. I was an agnostic and believed that we are just part of a continuum of life that began in prehistory under an extraordinary set of circumstances. Although I did not deny the existence of life after death, I had no comforting certainty that I would not just cease to exist at my death. Of this I was deeply afraid.

My life until that time had been comfortable and easy and I had never endured real hardship. But the Palestinians had. During the siege I witnessed their generosity and resilience. They shared with us what little food they had left. Young men died defending the camp. Women were shot trying to bring in food and medicine. From them I derived the courage to go on. So when I was asked on a small walkie-talkie whether we foreigners wanted to be "rescued," our answer was, "No." We were not prepared to abandon our patients, colleagues and friends to save our own skins.

I remain an agnostic and I am still afraid to die, but I have never regretted the decision not to leave. I learned that it is more important to uphold truth, to maintain dignity, to care about the well-being of others and to resist oppression than it is to preserve one's own life. The only immortality I believe we can achieve is through our interactions with our environment and those around us. Thus, the mark we leave, however big or small, good or bad, lives on after us.

Pauline Cutting,
British surgeon who has treated Palestinians in Lebanon and in the Israeli-occupied Gaza Strip, has received the Order of the British Empire.

It's been fifty years since Kristallnacht, the night Jewish synagogues and stores were destroyed in Germany and Austria. Hitler was testing the world to see how it reacted. And as we all know, the world didn't react. We are here to be vigilant, to be aware of the terrible things we can prevent—like the Holocaust, like Hiroshima, like hunger and want. There is a Jewish lullaby that says that we are like a river's shores, and deep, deep in us runs what has been, what we are now and what is to be transmitted to the next generation.

Ruth Westheimer,
sex therapist and psychologist, is known as television's Dr. Ruth.

My mother told me a story when I was a child. When Leo Tolstoy was an old man he was planting little apple trees. His neighbor laughed at him and called him a silly old man, because when the apples finally grew he wouldn't be around to eat them. Tolstoy told him, "Yes, but other people will eat them and they will think of me." I think that's what we're supposed to do: Leave more than we've found, give more than we've received, love more than we've been loved. And while we're here, we should always rewind the videotapes before returning them to the rental store.

Yakov Smirnoff,
comedian, is a Soviet émigré to the U.S.

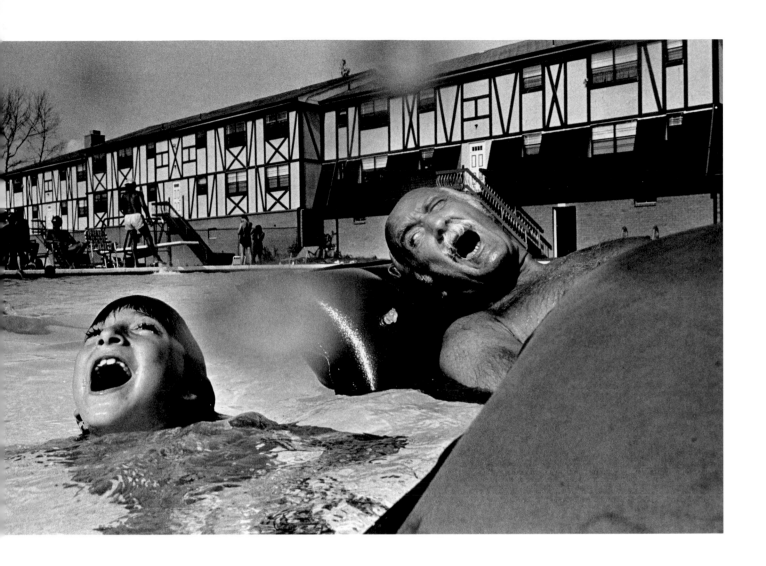

Sylvia Plachy
ISHI AND GRANDPA

Roswell Angie.
CHARLIE, JOAN AND JOAN'S MOTHE
NEW YORK CIT

"Why" is probably the most loaded, compact, incredible little three-letter word in all of language. Four-year-olds ask "Why?" constantly. Scientists and philosophers ponder "Why?" for hours and hours. The question "Why are we here?" poses a challenge for anyone to answer. Yet it is similar to the questions I am frequently asked as a triathlete. "Why do you spend all those hours training: swimming, cycling and running? Why do you participate in such a grueling sport?" My answer is: simply to glorify God. He has blessed me with the talents and abilities to race and train well. As a child of God, I live with a purpose: to honor Him who has given me this love for exercising, being outdoors amid His spectacular creation, and enjoying the people involved in the sport.

In athletics I have experienced everything from the thrill of victory—winning a world championship—to not competing and feeling the agony of injuries. But I have found that in Jesus Christ I am always victorious, I never really lose, and my identity is not based on how I perform. I am confident it is not by coincidence that we are here, but by God's purpose, design, love and creation. I have the privilege of living with Him and for Him. That's "Why!"

Kirsten Hanssen

a world champion triathlete.

We live in a pluralistic world comprised of multi-ethnic societies. Each nationality has its own religious beliefs based on its cultural background and historical traditions. However, despite these differences, every man invariably has the same overriding question: Is there purpose to the universe?

If we buy into the theory that we came in with a Big Bang and we're going out with a big fizzle, into the dust of nothingness, then life has no future. But as a born-again believer in Christ Jesus, I believe in the revealed Word of God—the Holy Bible.

Isaiah 43:7 says that man is created for the glory of God. Therefore the purpose that God has designed for man is to learn His will, to develop one's character in order to conform to His will, and to leave this world in better shape upon leaving it. The First Epistle of John 3:2 states: "Beloved, now are we the sons of God, and it doth not yet appear what we shall be; but we know that when he shall appear, we shall be like him." We are made *fully* in God's image. We should go about our Father's business: eradicating poverty, wiping out prejudice, lifting up our fellow man and living in peace one with another.

Shirley Caesar,

gospel singer, evangelist and outreach ministry founder, is a Pentacostal pastor.

I have life. With little effort on my behalf, apart from feeding my body, life pulsates through me. I have a body and a soul. I know that at some time physical life will be taken from me and my body will die. However, my soul, which has been created by God, can never die. By the power and mystery of God's grace, His spirit of love lives in every human soul. We are loved by God, and we are created to love God, to see the spirit of God in every person and to love and serve others.

There are many gifts that are given along with life, but the jewels among them are free will and love. With free will comes choice and responsibility. We must daily make very important choices. We can choose between life or death, good or evil, love or hate. We can choose to be creators or destroyers of life.

Personally, I choose to live. I know that my life—all human life—is sacred and precious. This means that I must never kill another person, and must reject personal and social violence. But it is not enough to refuse to kill. God's gift of love should open our hearts to see that the real enemies of humankind are disease, hunger, homelessness, torture, etc. These injustices we must work to change. Through active nonviolence we can work for justice, especially for the suffering and the poor. Through truth and love we can change ourselves, and our world, and come more deeply to know we are born to be loved and to love.

Mairead Maguire,

Irish peace activist and promoter of nonviolent protest, won the Nobel Peace Prize.

Life is not so much sweet as it is sacred.

The blues are not so much blue as they are bright.

And God is not so much just as She is right.

Basically life is pretty confusing. We come in screaming and go out screaming. And somewhere in between we try to figure out why we're here, what's on the other side of the veil, whether there *is* another side of the veil.

Sometimes it's damned interesting. You're totally alive with the idea that you've been chosen to be part of something miraculous. At other times it's the scariest thing in the world. You wake up at two or three in the morning and everything is still. And you realize then that the line between you and oblivion is a very thin one. It gives you a case of the shakes.

The Yoruba of southwestern Nigeria see the universe as created and controlled by one divine entity. That entity has many, many names and is composed of myriad Orisa—meaning, in the Yoruba language, "selected heads," repositories of divine soul force. Each thing in existence is of God and selected by God to share in His/Her universe. Every single blade of grass, cockroach, me, you were so chosen. We are all sacred.

John Mason,

Obatala priest, is director of the Yoruba Theological Archministry.

Life begins at conception when we choose our parents to be the vehicles to bring us here. We live here until we go back to the world we came from. Metaphysically, the world has three levels: physical, spiritual and mystical. We find life's meaning at each level. What gives life meaning is sharing—sharing bread, babies, moments, death, celebrations. It is recognizing that there is no separation between human beings or between human beings and the evolution of the world. Subconsciously and consciously, we are constantly expressing the fact that we are divine. We and the universe are evolving all the time; the only thing we can be sure of is change.

Naima Jody Sherwood

is a massage therapist.

My view of the meaning of life has been shaped by a large band of unusual and inadvertent adventurers. For ten years I have studied cases of persons who have survived episodes of near death or clinical death only to tell of wonders in the land *beyond* the edge of life.

One man speaks of being in a state of "total radiance from absolute knowledge" when he realized that "*finally* I was alive." One woman says: "I was enabled to look deeply inside myself. I saw . . . that my core was perfect love—and that applies to *all* human beings." But it is not just that one experiences this truth; one becomes it.

The meaning of life has something to do with realizing that our essence is perfect love, then going on to live our lives upon that truth, experiencing each day as a miracle and every act as sacred.

Kenneth Ring,

social psychologist, investigates near-death experiences.

Why are we here? To answer so lofty a question, many think we must study and write profound books such as this one. But the truth is far simpler. We must look right in front of us.

We are here to live and love the fullness of God's presence. But we need to stretch and train our abilities to recognize that presence. It isn't hidden in "holy places." Nor must experience of it arrive in great, blinding visions. God's presence awaits us everywhere. As scientists peer through microscopes . . . as parents delight in children's play . . . as vacationers watch the sun drop behind the horizon . . . as friends share hopes and fears, even suffering and death . . . as musicians compose a tune we can't forget . . . as wind rustles leaves, grass breaks ground, rivers turn a bend . . . as cats confound. In the sum total of such daily revelations lies not simply a formula for understanding life but an invitation to immerse ourselves in it. The meaning of life is something to be *experienced*.

Since all of us know the feeling of being "fully alive," we can take comfort that we all have access to the deepest experience of meaning. Another confirmation lies in our sense of joy. Yet another is the desire to share. God's presence is not for ourselves alone. Our impulse upon experiencing it is reach out to others, to include. In this spirit lies the foundation of justice: God's presence must be shared by *all*.

Meaning, then, is this presence of God among us, our individual birthright, available in all creation, discovered in the experience of life itself, confirmed by joy and grounded in justice. So read *The Meaning of Life*—but afterward, go live!

James Parks Morton,

dean of New York's Cathedral Church of St. John the Divine, is president of the Temple of Understanding, America's oldest interfaith organization.

Today is my birthday, probably the best time to consider the meaning of life. Looking back, I see that there has been no fixed purpose to attain. Meaning has been up to me to define. If I found the standards of society unappealing, I veered from them. If I found delight in private things, I preserved them. I set goals for myself. And as I achieved them, facing the conflicts between desire and reality, they defined what was important to me. Decisions about the future added still more significance.

I also experienced loss of meaning, where things that were once important became objects of indifference. I seldom felt that this showed the meaninglessness of existence. Rather, it was through this process that I learned detachment.

I believe that we are here to experience as much of ourselves and our world as we can before we die. The impassiveness that comes from long life is to be embraced, for that is the only way to look with unprejudiced eyes, the only way to joyously let go of civilization's trappings. We might say that the gradual and proper reduction of meaning, after a lifetime of fulfillment, is the purifying way to transcendence.

Deng Ming-Dao,
writer and martial artist, is
author of *The Wandering Taoist.*

To live a meaningful life, to be truthful to the life man has been given, man ought to be thankful for the life-producing and life-supporting powers around him: especially those of our ancestors, Nature itself and people living at all levels of the community. This duty comes from the Shintoist belief that two deities appeared sometime after the beginning of the universe and, in a human-like fashion, gave birth to many other deities including Nature, the lands of the earth and the Japanese people. The sun goddess— the highest and most gentle among these second-generation deities—advised her grandson to descend upon Japan and develop a peaceful nation, blessed in the knowledge that his descendants would be forever prosperous.

We are here on earth because of our ancestors' efforts. We must live a life that is grateful to the past and we must transmit our will to live to our descendants, as our ancestors did. In this way, the meaning of life will be fulfilled even though the earth and mankind may disappear sometime in the future.

Kenji Ueda,
Japanese educator, is a Shinto theologian.

From the time I could read, both my grandfather and father urged me to memorize Rudyard Kipling's poem "If—." It contained Kipling's vision of an ideal man, which, as an adult, I have changed, with due apologies to Kipling, to give the ideal man more concern and commitment. My version reads as follows:

In the garden of life, if you can be a
tiny seed,
    cast in the dirt to sprout;
If you can still grow tall and strong,
    and bear sweet, nourishing fruit
for others;
If you can exude an unforgettable
fragrance,
    through blossoms that enchant others;
If you can remain staunch and steadfast,
    through devastating storms;
If you can continue to spread goodness,
    while people hack at your limbs;
If you can be as useful in death as in life,
    as a tree decays and blankets the
forest's floor;
If you can move people to exclaim,
    "Oh what a giant that was!"
Then, my friend, life and its meaning
will no longer remain shrouded in mystery.

Arun Gandhi,
social activist who lectures on
civil rights and racial discrimination,
is the grandson of Mohandas Gandhi,
pioneer of nonviolent civil disobedience
who helped found modern India.

Raja Janaka, King of Mithila, had a dream in which he saw that he roamed the streets, begging for a piece of bread. As he cried out in the agony of hunger, he awoke. He rubbed his eyes and asked, "Am I a beggar dreaming that I am a king, or am I a king who dreamed he was a beggar? Which is true—this or that?"

He consulted wise men. Only one, Sage Ashtavakra, could give him a satisfactory answer: "Neither this is true nor that. You are neither a king nor a beggar. That you are a king is a dream; that you were a beggar was a dream within a dream!"

What, then, is the reality? What is the meaning of life? The meaning may not be expressed in words. It transcends the mind and the intellect. The meaning is to be experienced, *realized*. Realization is not the monopoly of a chosen few. It is open to everyone who would *live* according to certain disciplines. Three of the important ones are:

1. The discipline of *duty*. Life is a field of duty, not a dance of desires. Realization comes through performance of duties sincerely, honestly, earnestly, faithfully. What matters is not *what* we do, but *how* we do it.

2. The discipline of *service*. "Why are we here?" a boy asked his mother. She answered: "We are here to help others." Asked the boy, "What are the others here for, then?" The mother had no answer. He who would experience the meaning of life must not question this way. He must go about looking for opportunities to be of service to those in need. The opposite of love is not hate but apathy—indifference to the needs of others. The day we have not helped someone in need is a lost day, indeed.

3. The discipline of *silence*. Sit in your silence-corner, preferably at the same time and place, every day. It is your daily appointment with your true self. Pray, meditate, do your spiritual thinking. You will sink deeper and deeper within yourself until, one blessed day, you will behold a bright patch of light in your forehead. This will grow into a full orbit of light and your entire inner self will be illumined. And you, too, will experience that the meaning of life is to love God and to give the service of love to the suffering children of God. And to the birds and animals who are God's children as well.

J. P. Vaswani,
Hindu spiritual leader and author, heads India's Sadhu Vaswani Mission.

The Koran tells us that creation serves a just purpose and that Allah intended for self-conscious humanity, symbolized by Adam, to be the earthly *khalifa*, or deputy, of the universal Creator. Human beings who are made "in the best of molds" are capable of becoming Allah's co-workers in creating a temporal order that embodies divine attributes such as knowledge, justice, love and mercy. However, they are also capable of becoming the "lowest of the low" through misuse of the ability to think and exercise moral autonomy while doing that which is pleasing to Allah.

To me life is an internal and external journey toward attaining a state of peace that is the true goal of Islam. However, peace is not merely the absence of conflict even as health is not merely the absence of sickness.

According to the perspective of the Koran, peace is a positive state of safety or security in which one is free from anxiety or fear. It comes into being when human beings honoring the divine imperative to live justly, learn to be just to themselves and to others. Constant striving is required to overcome the fragmentation to which most human beings are subjected in the technological age. Constant striving is required to eliminate sexism, racism, classism and all forms of totalitarianism that lead to the injustices and inequities that characterize the world in which we live. To engage in such striving is the purpose of life.

Rifat Hassan,
native of Pakistan, is an Islamic scholar and feminist theologian.

A doctor's practice is to heal, but rarely is healing elevated to a belief. Twenty years ago I worked in the cancer wards of Boston hospitals. It was not lofty work; I was just a resident writing up routine physicals on patients who were dying—lonely people, many of them crushed, all of them in great pain far from home. If you had asked me the meaning of life, I would have said something grand and uplifting, but secretly I would have been thinking of them.

In the intervening years, my experience has been deeply influenced by Maharishi Mahesh Yogi and his technique of Transcendental Meditation. His teaching, rooted in the Vedic wisdom of many centuries, is that man is here to experience the unity of his own consciousness, to rise from suffering to perfection, and in the triumph of enlightenment to reclaim the earth as a heaven designed for him. Beneath the mask of suffering, the meaning of life is limitless freedom and the conquest of death.

I would never force these ideas on my patients, but many have learned to meditate, and now we are discovering the truth together. Lately I saw one of these patients, diagnosed with late-stage pancreatic cancer, eating quietly at the clinic. He turned to greet me, and my heart stopped to see the look of peace in his eyes. "Do you need anything?" I asked. "No," he said, "I'm okay." He was on no pain medication; he regarded his future, whatever it would be, with serenity. For me, the purpose of life is to help make this transformation possible.

Deepak Chopra,
endocrinologist and internist, is president of the Maharishi Ayurveda Association of America.

Alen MacWeeney
SORORITY SUNBATHERS, OLE MISS

oyce Ravid
DY

Frank Fournier
AIDS Victim Being Comforted
by Friend, New York City

184

In my mid-teens, on the way to a dance in my hometown in the Philippines, a friend then in medical school happened to be walking beside me and started to talk about a recent anatomy lesson. "As we were dissecting a human cadaver," he said, "I was watching the organs, the lungs, the heart and so on, seeing how they all functioned, complementing each other, to make up the living human organism. Suddenly it came to me. It's simply unthinkable that all *this* could spring out of mere chance."

Somehow his words struck a deep chord within me, and the dance that night had a different glow. It was held in an open-air courtyard, and the stars shone with a particular glitter. Every person on the dance floor seemed a precious jewel; each piece of music, every twist and jiggle joyous.

Years later Zen has helped clarify the significance of that heart-filling dance. Zen is, simply, the art of tasting. And we are here on earth to taste the wonder of every moment. Breathing in, breathing out. Have to go to the post office. Go to the post office. (Just that!) A friend is sick. Go visit her at the hospital. (Just that!) Hello, Maria. How are you today? (Just that!) Join a march to Hiroshima against nuclear weapons. (Every step, just that!)

Unthinkable . . . all *this* . . . mere chance!

Ruben Habito,
Filipino Catholic priest, is a Zen teacher.

B
Bound only by birth and death, life is both the ultimate mystery and the process of solving it. Life is a dance, a leap into the unknown. After you jump and before you land, is God. God is ecstasy: that state of being when everything comes together, nothing is missing, and it's all vibrating and electric. Life is an excuse for ecstasy, any way you can get it—in bed, in church, in a song.

Personally, I was born to die dancing.

Gabrielle Roth,
dancer and therapist, is the author of Maps to Ecstasy: Teachings of an Urban Shaman.

Kurt Markus
GREG LOUGANIS

The meaning of life comes in a flash. It is elusive and magical and lives in places that are hard to find. Once found, it transforms and exhilarates and validates life.

The process of transformation holds part of the meaning of life. This process can and does take place in music. The artful manipulation of vibrations allows us to travel in and out of our normal, waking states to explore and be nourished by the Muses.

Music is the sound track of life, "the music of the spheres." It is what life sounds like. If you have ears, you may hear the songs that men dance to, that magic moment when all events lead up to the creative flash, then explode in wonder, leaving us with the feeling that life is worthwhile, as it should be.

Mickey Hart,
who lectures on the music of different cultures, is the percussionist for the rock group The Grateful Dead.

L
Life has no meaning beyond this reality. But people keep searching for excuses. First there was reincarnation. Then refabrication. Now there's theories of life after amoebas, after death, *between* death, *around* death. Now you come back as a shirt, as a pair of pants. If Shirley MacLaine tells some brilliant guy, "There's an ethereal planet that sits right next to a delicatessen in Ethiopia and if you go shop there twice a day, you'll live forever," this *putz* believes it because he needs an answer from somebody. People call it truth, religion; I call it insanity, the denial of death as the basic truth of life. "What is the meaning of life?" is a stupid question. Life just exists. You say to yourself, "I can't accept that I mean nothing so I have to find the meaning of life so that I shouldn't mean as little as I know I do." Subconsciously you *know* you're full of s---. I see life as a dance. Does a dance have to have a meaning? You're dancing because you enjoy it.

Jackie Mason,
comedian, actor and former rabbi, won a Tony Award for his one-man Broadway show The World According to Me!

In 1974 I was blessed to have survived a brain aneurysm and two brain operations. It is unfortunate, but sometimes it takes a life-threatening crisis such as this to get your undivided attention, and this certainly did. I was given the opportunity to renew my basic belief in the importance of spirituality, reopening communications on a one-to-one basis with the Creator.

God has given each one of us approximately 25,000 to 26,000 days on this earth. I truly believe He (or She) has something very specific in mind: 8,300 days to sleep, 8,300 to work and 8,300 to give, live, play, pray and love one another.

We were born to struggle, to face the challenges of our lifetime and, ultimately, to evolve to a higher consciousness. When we find we can unyieldingly bestow our trust to that inner voice, it is evidence of our divine guidance.

The universal karmic law dictates: "You get what you give" and "You've got to bring some to get some." I would like to believe that the highest state of evolution in our lifetime is to reach a state where grace and giving reign and we experience the oneness of ourselves with the creations of this universe. We must search for the good in each of God's creations; it is important to invest our faith in the best part of humanity.

As songwriters Garrett and Ballard say in the Michael Jackson song "Man in the Mirror": If you wanna make the world a better place, take a look at yourself and make a change.

Quincy Jones,
record producer, is a composer, arranger and musician.

Geoffrey Biddle
207 EAST FIFTH STREET

The only real meaning in life can be found in a good man. And maybe Paris. Preferably the two together.

Marilyn vos Savant,
columnist and author, has
the world's highest I.Q. (230).

Robert Doisneau
BAISER DE L'HÔTEL DE VILLE

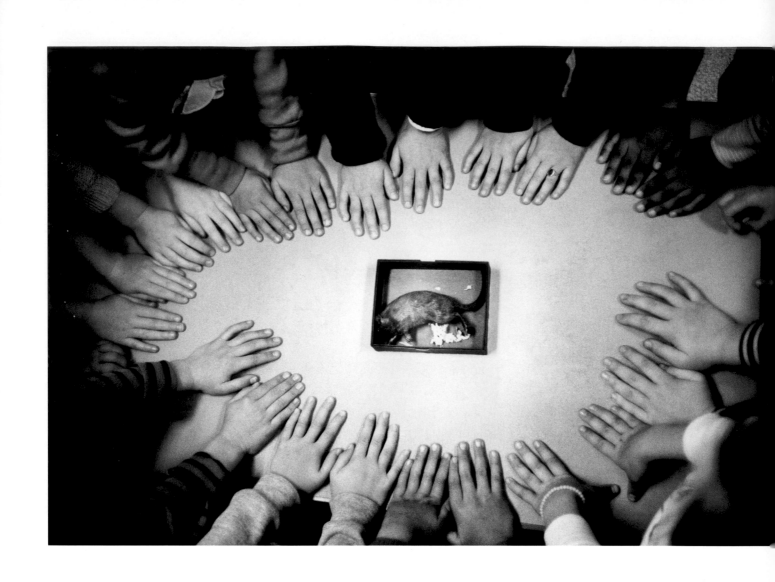

Donna Ferrato
DEATH OF THE CLASS GERBIL
UNITED NATIONS SCHOOL

ill Freedman
EARL QUEEN AND THE PEANUT GALLERY,
EW ORLEANS

Some contend that we are here only by chance, as stepping-stones in the evolution of the species. Others insist that our lives are predestined by a divine will. I cannot accept either of these extremes because they are based on the false premise that we have no control of our destiny.

Unless a person has a reason to live, he dies—first mentally and then physically. Self-gratification is not an adequate reason to live. Only a life lived for others is worth living. We cannot live a full life unless we have a purpose bigger than ourselves. We all cannot expect to be great philosophers, scientists, statesmen or business leaders. But we must always seek to reach up and reach out to achieve our full potential. Some of the most heroic lives are lived by those who cope with the tragedy, adversity and daily drudgery of life and rise above it. It is a mistake to assume that we can ever achieve perfection. But it is an even greater mistake to cease trying. Without risk there will be neither success nor failure. As Thomas Aquinas observed: If the primary aim of a captain were to preserve his ship, he would keep it in port forever.

Richard Nixon

is the thirty-seventh President
of the United States.

I have always been extremely puzzled by those who have claimed that if there is no God, then life is meaningless. Is there the slightest shred of evidence that secular humanists find life less meaningful than do religious believers? I am not claiming that there is no God, nor am I claiming that there is one. All I am claiming is that life is extremely meaningful to most of those who live it—God or no God!

I cannot help but think of the marvelous haiku: "Quite apart from our religion, there are plum blossoms; there are cherry blossoms."

Raymond Smullyan

is a mathematical logician, essayist
and creator of puzzles.

Life has neither material nor idealistic secrecy or mystery about it. Life is equal to itself only, hence perceiving its meaning is out of the question. Never will we get to the bottom of this whole business and learn the meaning of life, love, death, beauty, poetry, because they just exist. Noncognizability is in some sense the most universal law of life. The exaggeration of our mental abilities has given rise to what we perceive as "the problem" of discerning life's purpose.

In my twenty-seventh year, while riding the metro in Leningrad, I was overcome with a despair so great that life seemed to stop at once, preempting the future entirely, let alone any meaning. Suddenly, all by itself, a phrase appeared: Without God life makes no sense. Repeating it in astonishment, I rode the phrase up like a moving staircase, got out of the metro and into God's light and carried on living.

Faith is the only truth and the rarest of gifts. Exaggeration without faith is dangerous whether man recognizes the existence of God or denies it. If man does recognize it, his misinterpreting leads him down the path of idolatry so that he ends up idolizing both the random and the particular. If man denies God, he is certain to take the particular for the whole and the random for the regular, becoming imprisoned by the logic of denial.

The more convincing the explanation of life's purpose, the more private it becomes. Taken for granted as a guide to action, an espoused purpose leads to ideological crimes. The idea of predestation is tempting, imbuing life with significance and purpose. Giving away no clues, predestination *leads* man along the road of life.

But if it is beyond our powers to disembowel love and beauty—we can only ravish them—it means that they are given to us not for cognition but for reflection. Similarly, the freedom of choice granted to man, a freedom denied the rest of the living species, is man's task, a duty to exercise and fulfill, not merely an opportune option.

Andrei Bitov

is a Soviet novelist, short-story
writer and editor.

To understand the meaning of life consider the argument of scientific humanism, which goes as follows: If two explanations work equally well, take the one that is simpler. With this in mind, it is fair to say that biology has advanced to the point of questioning the need for purpose in human existence beyond that created autonomously during human evolution. This is not to claim that no such purpose exists, only that it is not required explain what we know about human existence. A human being is assembled by the inner workings of about 100,000 genes. These informational units change by random chemical reactions called mutations; they form new ensembles by sexual recombination; and, finally, they spread or decline by natural selection. Evolution by mutation and natural selection is a relentlessly dynamic and creative process. It combines elements of chance (the mutations) and survival in a constantly changing environment. Almost all biologists feel certain that life as we know it has arisen by evolution. In addition many scientists and philosophers—the scientific humanists—believe that the human brain and all its activities have arisen from the same earthbound, autonomous process. Hence, no more complicated explanation is needed to account for human existence, either scientifically or spiritually. Maybe the cosmos was set in motion by a higher intelligence but life down here was left alone to run its own course.

Where does this leave us? We can gain comfort by believing in divine guidance, but in matters of the greatest importance we will be more prudent to depend on all the material knowledge and wisdom that humanity can summon up.

Edward Wilson,

zoologist, sociobiologist
and Pulitzer Prize-winning
author, wrote *On Human Nature.*

We believe what we want to believe, that which satisfies us best, i.e., every belief is a superstition. Purposes evolve from men's needs. We call these purposes "designs"; that life should have a purpose is a man-made proposition and our theories about this we call "grand designs."

These two observations interrelate as neatly as the components of any pagan symbol of the world. They are essentially the components of philosophy from the skeptical viewpoint. Philosophy is anthropocentric.

If one wished to choose one's "purposes" according to reason, one would seek to base opinion on what would seem to be fact rather than on emotion. One would make judgments based on awareness rather than being subject to prejudice. If many wished to do this, then the world would change and the power of government to manipulate opinion by appealing to emotion would be in jeopardy. We would have art instead of war. We would have civilization. The most dangerous threat to this model of civilization has been the idea that mind and matter are separate. There has never been any scientific evidence to support the idea that matter is a product of mind but all science supports the opposite, that mind is a product of matter. All evidence of extrasensory phenomena, instinct, an individual's sense of his own anima and his ability to communicate spiritually with others is part of intelligence. Appreciation of nondual reality is as beneficial to our possible civilized world as the ozone layer. Man-made indulgence in duality destroys.

Vivienne Westwood,
British designer, has been called the mother of punk fashion.

For the less fortunate, hunger creates meaning, as does poverty. Or war. Or oppression. For those raised above Abraham Maslow's level of "basic needs," innate compassion urges humans to take note of comparative circumstance—a deep-seated desire that creates meaning when fulfilled.

For most civilized peoples, belonging provides definition and thereby gives meaning. Thus, the most obvious way that we create meaning for ourselves, however unwittingly, is in the groups to which we belong, by choice or otherwise. Moreover, people sense a social contract with each belonging, explicit or not, an obligation to contribute to the raison d'être of the group. How strongly we associate and how well we fulfill this often unconscious obligation determine how much meaning we find.

Religion provides a sense of belonging for many, although unfortunately this often amounts to a belief in religion that can overshadow a belief in God. I believe that on a spiritual level, the key to meaning lies in the ability to be comfortable with one's uncertainty about the form assumed by God or the universe. It is sufficient to know that giving with love to those you encounter is all that any God you might define desires.

Jonathan Bender
is a video executive.

The aim of life is to prove a conjecture (for a mathematician it's to do mathematics, for an artist it's to paint) and to keep the s.f. score low. This is a joke, of course. The s.f. is the Supreme Fascist or, in other words, God. The game of life is played as follows: If you do something bad, then the s.f. scores at least two points. If you don't do something good that you could have done, then the s.f. scores at least one point. And *you never score*. The aim of the game is to keep the s.f. score as low as possible. And if you assume the s.f. is good, that God is good, then you can think of it as: The s.f. wants the score kept low. But for reasons that we can't fully fathom, he's not supposed to intervene.

Paul Erdös,
Hungarian professor, is often considered the world's most prolific mathematician.

What are we doing here? Trying to understand just that. Except we do it poorly. We often lack courage to grapple with the issue, getting ourselves preoccupied with daily pursuits as we keep pressing on blindly. This, among other things, results in workaholic escapism, which accounts for a good deal of human endeavor.

For all we know, we hardly asked to be born. Was this gift of life bestowed upon us as a responsibility? An obligation to seek our true self? A commitment to solitary striving, to move from wherever they got us started to someplace else, making it possible for those who'll follow us to continue once we've stopped? Life is a tough job not everyone can cope with. Some gift. But, then again, it's bad manners to look a gift horse in the mouth.

Maybe the awareness of this commitment to evolve, to reach beyond ourselves—an awareness we can't really identify in terms of human thinking or express in terms of human speech—is the only real glimpse of the meaning of life we're entitled to. But this awareness alone makes it possible for our spiritual development as humans.

Life, however, is not meant to be wasted in scholastic theorizing about its meaning. It is meant to be lived: lived by trial and error, which, though not an altogether reasonable process, seems somehow humane nonetheless. Life hasn't been meted out to us as a blueprint to be unflinchingly followed. Life is a matter of choice, left entirely up to us.

Choose your best.

Yuri Zarakhovich
is a Soviet translator.

Alex Webb
Ciudad Madero, Mexico

(Overleaf)
Gilles Peress
French Peasants,
Merdrignac, Brittany

197

Copernicus decentered the earth, Darwin relativized the godlike image of man, Marx exploded the ideology of social harmony and Freud complicated our conscious life. They have redefined humanity for the modern age. Yet they have also empowered us, with communal, critical self-awareness, to renew our faith in the ancient Confucian wisdom that the globe is the center of our universe and the only home for us and that we are the guardians of the good earth, the trustees of the mandate of heaven that enjoins us to make our bodies healthy, our hearts sensitive, our minds alert, our souls refined and our spirits brilliant.

We are here because embedded in our human nature is the secret code for heaven's self-realization. Heaven is certainly omnipresent, may even be omniscient, but is most likely not omnipotent. It needs our active participation to realize its own truth. We are heaven's partners, indeed cocreators. We serve heaven with common sense, the lack of which nowadays has brought us to the brink of self-destruction. Since we help heaven to realize itself through our self-discovery and self-understanding in day-to-day living, the ultimate meaning of life is found in our ordinary, human existence.

Tu Wei-ming,

professor of Chinese history and philosophy, is a Confucian scholar.

I no longer ask the young man's question: How far will I go? My questions are now those of the mature person: When it is over, what will my life have been about? First, as Martin Buber taught, life is meeting. We come alive only when we relate to others. Secondly, we are here to change the world with small acts of thoughtfulness done daily rather than with one great breakthrough. Finally, we are here to finish God's labors. One of the sages of the Talmud taught nearly two thousand years ago that God could have created a plant that would grow loaves of bread. Instead He created wheat for us to mill and bake into bread. Why? So that we could be His partners in completing the work of creation.

Harold Kushner,

rabbi, is the author of *When Bad Things Happen to Good People.*

I would never compromise my faith by accepting any of the bio-theories that originated with the Darwinian theory of evolution, theories that have not been verified or affirmed by paleontological or archeological findings or even by the observations of the universe that modern-day astronauts and astronomers have been able to make. In my opinion, men and women are here for only one purpose and, for that matter, the most sublime purpose: to try to re-create life in its original form by restoring beauty and order in their individual lives and by continuously striving to achieve the common dream of one world community, free of pollution and ugliness, before war, starvation, discord and crime destroy the last hope of the world.

According to Genesis 1:26-28, human life was created by God in His image and likeness in order for men and women to be fruitful, to multiply, to fill the earth and conquer it, which means, in effect, that we must master and direct our destiny.

We are here, therefore, to continue God's creative work and give to life its true meaning: to arrive at His image and likeness and turn the world into a loving society of men and women.

Archbishop Iakovos

is primate of the Greek Orthodox Church of North and South America.

What is the meaning of life? Life is for the absolute satisfaction of God the Creator and God the Creation.

The meaning of life is to become inseparably one with God the transcendental Bliss and God the universal Peace.

The meaning of life is to achieve unconditional self-giving and a self-giving will, at God's choice Hour, in the unhorizoned blossoming of God-becoming.

Life means willpower, the willpower that unites God's descending Compassion-Smile with man's ascending aspiration-cry. In the desire-bound life, there are teeming rules and regulations. In the aspiration-free life, there is only one rainbow-rule: complete faith in oneself and birthless and deathless faith in God.

Life is love: animal love, human love and divine love. Animal love is destruction. Human love is frustration. Divine love is satisfaction. Again, love is life par excellence because it is the existence-reality itself.

Life needs a dream and a goal. Today's dream and goal have to be transcended tomorrow. Each Himalayan dream of man is God's own Self-Transcendence.

Transcendence is the glorious beginning of human perfection. Perfect perfection is pure satisfaction within and sure satisfaction without.

What is the meaning of life and who am I? From time immemorial these two questions have remained inseparably one. Who am I? I am my life's unfinished God-manifestation.

Sri Chinmoy,

Indian guru, is an athlete, world-class weight-lifter and musician.

Jerry Gordon

THE BREAKERS HOTEL
PALM BEACH, FLORIDA

Gordon Parks
Bessie Fontenelle and Children at
the Welfare Office, New York

(Overleaf)
Anonymous/U.S. Army
AMERICAN POWs FREED FROM
GERMAN PRISON CAMP,
WORLD WAR II

Lynn Johnson
DAY-CARE MOM, ST. LOUIS

We are here to be excited from youth to old age, to have an insatiable curiosity about the world. Aldous Huxley once said that to carry the spirit of the child into old age is the secret of genius. And I buy that. We are also here to genuinely, humbly and sincerely help others by practicing a friendly attitude. And every person is born for a purpose. Everyone has a God-given potential, in essence, built into them. And if we are to live life to its fullest, we must realize that potential.

Norman Vincent Peale,
Protestant pastor, wrote
The Power of Positive Thinking.

John Loengard
PHOTOGRAPHER HENRI CARTIER-BRESSON
FLIES KITE IN THE SOUTH OF FRANCE

(Overleaf)
Ken Heyman
SICILY

Ralph Sumner died the other day, full of years (eighty plus) and wisdom (dairy farmer, cabinetmaker, churchgoer, member of the local road crew, dowser). When we laid him in the ground there were some tears, but there was also a lot of gratitude for the joy he had spread around the folk of Heath, MA 01346. Ralph's death made me think about my life.

I believe we are placed here to be companions—a wonderful word that comes from *cum panis* ("with bread"). We are here to share bread with one another so that everyone has enough, no one has too much and our social order achieves this goal with maximal freedom and minimal coercion. There are many names for such sharing: utopia, the beloved community, the Kingdom of God, the communion of saints. And while the goal is too vast to be realized solely on this planet, it is still our task to create foretastes of it on this planet—living glimpses of what life is *meant* to be, which include art and music and poetry and shared laughter and picnics and politics and moral outrage and special privileges for children only and wonder and humor and endless love, to counterbalance the otherwise immobilizing realities of tyrants, starving children, death camps and just plain greed.

But I expect Ralph Sumner now sees it more clearly than I do.

Robert McAfee Brown,
Presbyterian minister and educator, is a professor of theology and ethics.

Why are we here? Who are *we*? Where *is* here? *Which* here?

As a species of unfathomably diverse individuals we seem to be engaged in a vast experiment of consciousness: the evolution of consciousness. As individuals, we seem to be engaged in "lives" that might be seen as sequences of problem-solving episodes giving pain and pleasure in varying doses. As family members, we seem to be engaged in creating and sustaining fragile, yet powerful, auras of love.

But maybe we are here simply to tell stories to one another about why we're here, and where we're headed. Aristotle speculated that imagination springs from desire; desiring something not-us, not-here, we create *phantasia*—the mind telling itself stories. All religions are the consequence of elaborate, communally shared fantasies, ingenious efforts of storytelling. And why not, if the stories yield pleasure?

The nicest and shortest answer might be this: We're here to feel the joy of life pulsing in us—now.

Joyce Carol Oates
is an essayist, poet, novelist and short-story writer.

Our purpose is to consciously, deliberately evolve toward a wiser, more liberated and luminous state of being; to return to Eden, make friends with the snake and set up our computers among the wild apple trees.

Deep down, all of us are probably aware that some kind of mystical evolution is our true task. Yet we suppress the notion with considerable force because to admit it is to admit that most of our political gyrations, religious dogmas, social ambitions and financial ploys are not merely counterproductive but trivial. Our mission is to jettison those pointless preoccupations and take on once again the primordial cargo of inexhaustible ecstasy. Or, barring that, to turn out a good, juicy cheeseburger and a strong glass of beer.

Tom Robbins,
novelist, is the author of *Even Cowgirls Get the Blues.*

No why. Just here.

John Cage,
avant-garde composer, is a writer, philosopher and musical innovator.

Leonard Freed
HARLEM SUMMER DAY

(Overleaf)
René Burri
LOTUS FLOWERS IN THE LAKE OF THE SUMMER PALACE, BEIJING

211

Contributors

72 **M**ortimer Adler

20 **M**aya Angelou

195 **J**onathan Bender

100 **J**oan Borysenko

124 **W**illiam Burroughs — BOB ADELMAN

20 **S**ally Casper

118 **T**ania Aebi

65 **M**ichéle August

194 **A**ndrei Bitov

121 **B**arbara Brennan

21 **R**ichard Bushman

118 **F**rank Chin

86 **M**uhammad Ali

143 **G**ae Aulenti — GIUSEPPE PINO

127 **H**arry Blackmun

211 **R**obert McAfee Brown

177 **S**hirley Caesar

181 **D**eepak Chopra

21 **C**leveland Amory

146 **E**laine Barnes

93 **P**aul Bocuse

39 **C**harles Bukowski — LINDA BUKOWSKI

211 **J**ohn Cage — ROGER GORDY

64 **R**aymond Clark

143 **L**ynn Andrews

110 **W**ilfred Beckerman

100 **J**ean Shinoda Bolen

135 **C**atharine Burroughs

21 **H**elen Caldicott

72 **A**rthur C. Clarke

93	**64**	**64**	**76**	**126**	**126**
Flora Colao	**C**hris DeMatteo	**W**endy Doniger	**F**alaka Fattah	**P**eter Gay	**R**onald Graham
146	**180**	**39**	**86**	**27**	**152**
William Cook	**D**eng Ming-Dao	**F**rank Donofrio	**B**etty Friedan	**R**ichard Gere	**G**ustavo Gutierrez
118	**49**	**87**	**169**	**86**	**187**
Harvey Cox	**J**enna de Rosnay	**A**ndrea Dworkin	**J**ason Gaes	**N**ed Gillette	**R**uben Habito
16	**16**	**195**	**174**	**20**	**29**
Charles Curran	**L**eah de Roulet	**P**aul Erdös	**E**duardo Galeano	**D**exter Gordon	**A**rmand Hammer
174	**11**	**127**	**180**	**33**	**177**
Pauline Cutting	**A**nnie Dillard	**E**mil Fackenheim	**A**run Gandhi	**S**tephen Jay Gould	**K**irsten Hanssen
49	**65**	**104**	**141**	**104**	**93**
The Dalai Lama	**M**ike Ditka	**J**erry Falwell	**S**hakti Gawain	**B**illy Graham	**C**harles Harbutt

SUSAN WOOD 85

DAVID S. JOHNSON

HECTOR ZAMPAGLIONE © 1987

CAROL FRIEDMAN / 1986

110 Michael Harrington | 39 Jenny Holzer | 104 D. E. Jenkins | 82 Chaka Khan | 105 Hans Küng | 65 Maya Lin

187 Mickey Hart | 107 Thomas Hopko | 69 Donald Johanson | 51 Jamaica Kincaid | 200 Harold Kushner | 107 Georgi Litichevsky

181 Rifat Hassan | 16 Derek Humphry | 187 Quincy Jones | 102 J. Z. Knight | 55 Gary Lamb | 117 Robert Longo

121 Theodore Hesburgh | 200 Archbishop Iakovos | 124 Firuz Kazemzadeh | 126 Sergei Kovalyov | 62 Timothy Leary | 45 George Lucas

146 Lynn Hill-Raffa | 76 Jesse Jackson | 39 Amy Keim | 160 Marc Kravitz | 147 Madeleine L'Engle | 76 Alma Lyons

124 Jeffrey Hoffman | 72 Julian Jaynes | 100 Wolfe Kelman | 65 Elisabeth Kübler-Ross | 86 Rita Levi-Montalcini | 177 Mairead Maguire

13 Wilma Mankiller

13 Michael McCloskey — JAN GAUTHIER

194 Richard Nixon — BEN MARTIN

27 Raimon Panikkar

149 Jacquie Phelan — SCOTT R. HINRICHS

65 Ishmael Reed

93 Serin Marshall

165 James Merrill

86 Oliver North

87 Rosa Parks

19 Carmine Pucci

178 Kenneth Ring

121 Martin Marty

118 Sun Myung Moon

211 Joyce Carol Oates

69 Linus Pauling

146 Joan Quigley

211 Tom Robbins

187 Jackie Mason

178 James Parks Morton

20 Thomas E. O'Connor

207 Norman Vincent Peale

117 Ram Dass

187 Gabrielle Roth — © 1988 LISA LAW PRODUCTIONS

178 John Mason

62 Seyyed Hossein Nasr

146 Seiji Ozawa

64 Maggi Peirce

127 Judith Rapoport

36 Todd Rundgren

95 Marlee Matlin — ROBERT COHEN

49 Willie Nelson — BEVERLY PARKER

72 Cynthia Ozick — JULIUS OZICK

127 H. Ross Perot

147 Robert Rauschenberg

73 Carl Sagan

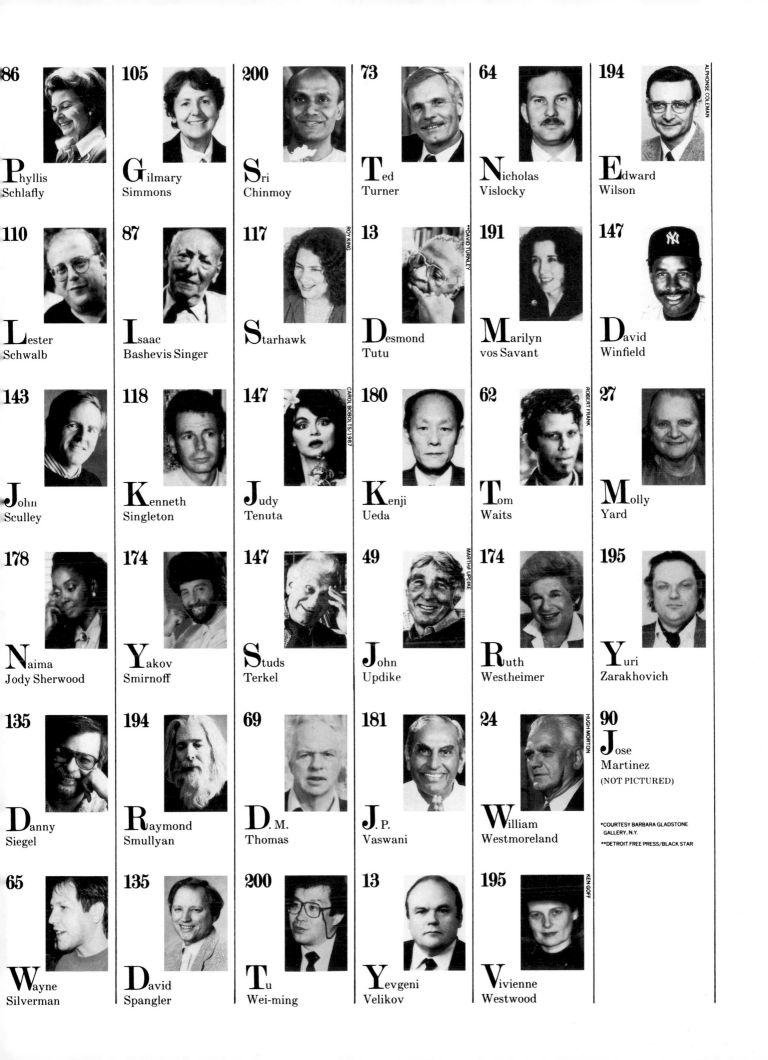

86 Phyllis Schlafly

105 Gilmary Simmons

200 Sri Chinmoy

73 Ted Turner

64 Nicholas Vislocky

194 Edward Wilson

ALPHONSE COLEMAN

110 Lester Schwalb

87 Isaac Bashevis Singer

117 Starhawk

ROY KING

13 Desmond Tutu

"DAVID TURNLEY

191 Marilyn vos Savant

147 David Winfield

143 John Sculley

118 Kenneth Singleton

147 Judy Tenuta

CAROL BOBOLTS/1987

180 Kenji Ueda

62 Tom Waits

ROBERT FRANK

27 Molly Yard

178 Naima Jody Sherwood

174 Yakov Smirnoff

147 Studs Terkel

49 John Updike

MARTHA UPDIKE

174 Ruth Westheimer

195 Yuri Zarakhovich

135 Danny Siegel

194 Raymond Smullyan

69 D. M. Thomas

181 J. P. Vaswani

24 William Westmoreland

HUGH MORTON

90 Jose Martinez (NOT PICTURED)

*COURTESY BARBARA GLADSTONE GALLERY, N.Y.

**DETROIT FREE PRESS/BLACK STAR

65 Wayne Silverman

135 David Spangler

200 Tu Wei-ming

13 Yevgeni Velikov

195 Vivienne Westwood

KEN GOFF

Photographers

Abbas 71

Adelman, Bob 98

Alexanian, Nubar 10

Allen, Jules 108

Angier, Roswell 176

Anonymous/American
    Red Cross 114

Anonymous/U.S. Army 204

Asher, Louise 112

Baltermants, Dmitri 132

Barboza, Anthony 151

Baughman, J. Ross 58

Bazan, Ernesto 162

Benson, Harry 22

Biddle, Geoffrey 188

Birns, Jack 67

Blue, Patt 50

Brandenburg, Jim 75

Bryson, John 46

Burnett, David 152

Burri, René 212

Burrows, Larry 28

Callahan, Harry 113

Capa, Cornell 158

Capa, Robert 170

Challenger 6, 41 G Space
    Shuttle Crew/NASA 12

Cobb, Jodi 44

Coster, Gordon 54

Cowans, Adger 74

Crane, Ralph 96

Da Miano, André 130

Davidson, Bruce 163

Davis, Myron H. 92

De Roy, Tui 32

Doisneau, Robert 190

Dominis, John 84

Duke, Charles/NASA, 47

Eisenstaedt, Alfred 6, 8

Erwitt, Elliott 128

Feinstein, Harold 48

Fermilab, 30

Ferorelli, Enrico 154

Ferrato, Donna 192

Fink, Larry 136

Fournier, Frank 184

Frajndlich, Abe 109

Freed, Leonard 210

Freedman, Jill 193

Gibson, Ralph 36

Goldman, Robert 68

Goldsmith, Lynn 106

Gordon, Jerry 201

Graves, Ken 221

Griffiths, Philip Jones 42

Haley, Tom 24

Halmi, Robert 56

Harbutt, Charles 102

Heyman, Abigail 185

Heyman, Ken 7, 208

Hoffman, Ethan 111

Hurn, David 168

Jacobson, Jeff 85

Johnson, Lynn 203

Josephson, Kenneth 196

Koudelka, Josef 145

Kubota, Hiroji 164

Kuehn, Karen 138

Lanker, Brian 66

Liftin, Joan 134

Loengard, John 206

MacWeeney, Alen 182

Mapplethorpe, Robert 15

Mark, Mary Ellen 160

Markus, Kurt 186

Marshall, Jim 41

McCullin, Don 52

McNally, Joe 119

Mehta, Dilip 144

Meiselas, Susan 99

Menashe, Abraham 94

Metzner, Dolores 139

Meyerowitz, Joel 140

Michals, Duane 63

Miller, Francis 79

Misrach, Richard 40

Morabito, Rocco 77

Morse, Ralph 142

Muench, David 116

Mydans, Carl 81

Nachtwey, James 43

Nichols, Michael K. 78

Nilsson, Lennart 14

O'Brien, Michael 156

O'Neill, Michael 88

Orkin, Ruth 70

Owens, Bill 137

Parks, Gordon 202

Peress, Gilles 198

Plachy, Sylvia 175

Ravid, Joyce 183

Reed, Eli 171

Reininger, Alon 34

Rentmeester, Co 148

Riboud, Marc 61

Richards, Eugene 129

Robertson, Grace 101

Salgado, Sebastião 166

Sanders, Thomas 125

Schatz, Arthur 120

Seymour, David 172

Sherman, Cindy 155

Shunk, Harry 38

Siegel, Larry 60

Smith, W. Eugene 157

Starn Twins 150

Steber, Maggie 80

Sund, Harald 179

Swannell, John 82

Tarasevich, Vsevolod 18

Tenneson, Joyce 131

Tress, Arthur 26

Turnley, David 59

Uzzle, Burke 122

Villet, Grey 17

Webb, Alex 197

Winogrand, Garry 189

Zecchin, Franco 90

PICTURE SOURCES

American Red Cross *114*

Black Star *7, 59, 96,
    192, 203, 208*

Contact Press Images *34,
    144, 152, 184*

JB Pictures *80*

LGI Photo Agency *106*

Magnum Photos Inc. *42, 43,
    52, 61, 71, 78, 90, 99, 128,
    129, 145, 163, 164, 166,
    168, 171, 172, 197, 198,
    210, 212*

NASA *12, 47*

National Geographic
    Society *44, 75*

Sipa Press *24*

Sygma *109*

U.S. Army *204*

Visions Photo Inc. *58*

*page 68: Robert Goldman photograph
courtesy Department of Cell Biology and
Anatomy, Northwestern University
Medical School, Chicago*

*page 186: Kurt Markus photograph
courtesy Esquire magazine*

Ken Graves
PIANO RECITAL, SAN FRANCISCO

THIS BOOK IS TYPESET IN MODERN NO. 1 AND MODERN NO. 20
AND PRINTED BY ACME PRINTING COMPANY, INC., WILMINGTON, MASSACHUSETTS.